Mr Wright

THE EXPLOSIVE AUTOBIOGRAPHY OF IAN WRIGHT

CollinsWillow
An Imprint of HarperCollinsPublishers

To Tony Davies and Errol Palmer of
Ten Em Bee Football Club

First published in 1996
by CollinsWillow
an imprint of HarperCollins*Publishers*
London

3 5 7 9 8 6 4 2

A CIP catalogue record for this book is
available from the British Library

ISBN 0 00 218726 4

Printed in Great Britain by
Caledonian International Book Manufacturing Ltd, Glasgow

Contents

Introduction

When you've got up at six o'clock in the morning to go to work and it's pitch black outside, and you know it will still be dark when you come home at night, that's when you appreciate being a professional footballer.

And when you've worked in freezing ankle-deep water with stinking chemicals that can strip your skin, then you know just how lucky you are to play football for a living. And when you've seen the inside of a prison cell, been locked up for twenty hours a day and marched round a prison courtyard, then you know you've been blessed that God has given you the chance to make something of your life through a sport that you love.

I'm not saying that I'm special, because I respect any person who goes out to work twelve hours a day to feed their family and give them a home, but I've experienced the other side of life away from football, so I know just what a privilege it is to become well-off doing a job you love. Perhaps that's why people say I'm too intense on the pitch, that I care too much sometimes. Too right I care, because I know just how far I've come through football and I don't want anybody to take that away from me.

Bruce Rioch told me that I should play every game as if it was my last, so that people would go away from a match and say, 'I saw Ian Wright play today and it was worth every penny of the price.' To me, that sums up what my life as a professional sportsman is all about. It's about pride and about doing the right thing every step of the way. Football makes millions of people happy every day, and players should always remember the debt that they owe the fans who come to watch them every week. I know I do.

Ian Wright

1
Should I Stay or Should I Go?

My love affair with Arsenal was over. Everything that I had built up over the previous five years was about to collapse and I knew that I had to get away from Highbury for my own sake and the club's, otherwise my career would be heading in only one direction – downhill.

Those were my feelings when I handed in a transfer request in February 1996. I thought I had reached the end of the road and gone as far as I could go with Arsenal, and the best thing for everybody concerned would be if I left immediately. It was the hardest decision I'd ever had to take in my life, let alone football, and in the weeks leading up to it I struggled to get to sleep, constantly going over and over in my mind what a massive step I was taking.

Looking back now, it makes me sick to think that I came so close to throwing away everything I'd worked so hard for. If the people who I respect at Arsenal hadn't been so patient and understanding, I could have found myself out on my ear and not playing for the greatest club in Britain. Every time I think of those dreadful days in February, all I hear are George Graham's words coming back to haunt me. He used to drill into us just how great a club Arsenal is, that people who left Highbury regretted it instantly and we should always realise just how lucky we were. He used to say, 'You might think the grass is greener elsewhere, but just walk away from here and you'll see nothing matches up to Arsenal.'

Thank God I never found out if George's words were true, but I'll tell you something, I came too damn close. At the time I felt justified because so many things were going on and, for the first time in my Arsenal career, I felt unwanted and almost taken for granted. I know now that I overreacted and perhaps I let my heart rule my head, but at the time I was so depressed.

The crazy thing is that 1995/96 had all the makings of a great season. There was a new regime at the club, a new manager, a wonderful feeling of confidence and self-belief and to top it all off, suddenly, within the space of a month, we had signed two of the biggest names in world football.

Everybody thought then when I handed in my transfer request that it was simply for one reason – that I didn't get on with Bruce Rioch. I have to be honest, and I'm sure Bruce would be the first to admit it as well, that we didn't exactly have the best of relationships in his first season at Highbury. We both said things that shouldn't have been said and we had more than our fair share of bust-ups, but in the cold light of day I know he was only doing what he thought best for Arsenal Football Club.

As soon as George Graham got the sack and it was made clear that Stewart Houston wasn't going to get the job, it seemed like the whole world and its wife was up for the Arsenal manager's job. Many names were thrown around, men like Bobby Robson, Ray Harford and several foreign coaches, but the one person who got more mentions than most was Bruce Rioch, so when he was appointed it didn't exactly come as a shock.

Bruce had done a great job at Bolton and I know that his attitude impressed the Arsenal board. They felt they needed somebody who would take the club into a new era, a manager with a lot of respect within the game and, more importantly, someone with no skeletons and the correct image. The club had just gone through the worst season in its history as far as scandals were concerned, and I suppose the directors felt they had to start the new season whiter than white.

I'd heard all about Bruce because as soon as a new manager is appointed, the soccer grapevine goes into overdrive and you get everybody in the world phoning to either tell you something about the new boss or ask about him. He had a reputation as a disciplinarian and people immediately assumed that we'd be at each other's throats from the moment he stepped through the door! I'm not sure what people thought about George Graham, but one thing I can tell you, he wasn't a soft touch. You knew where you stood with him and if you stepped over the line, then you'd get slapped down, and when George slapped you down you stayed slapped.

So if anybody thought that I'd have a problem with Bruce's discipline and authority, then they were mistaken. All I wanted to do was play football, do my stuff on the pitch and keep myself to myself off it.

I was having treatment at Highbury the day the club threw a press conference to announce Bruce as the new manager. As I was walking down the corridor, I bumped into him and immediately we threw our arms round each other, had a few pictures done and then had a quick chat. He impressed me with his manner and the way he put his ideas across; there was something really positive about him and he obviously had big plans for the club and was determined to put them straight into operation.

I left that day feeling on a high, like somebody had come along and given me a massive boost of confidence. After the dark days of the previous season when the world was crashing down around our ears, at least I could see real daylight and I was excited. I was also looking forward to having a great holiday in Sardinia with my great mate, Paul Ince and his family before coming back refreshed for the new season and really doing the business.

I didn't have much contact with Bruce throughout the rest of the close season, but I didn't need to speak to him to be even more impressed, all I had to do was read the back pages of the newspapers every day. Suddenly, from being a club that was always left behind in the transfer market when it came to the biggest names, we were right there at the front of the pack. If a star player was up for grabs, then we'd be linked with him. All the rumours of a wage ceiling were blown out of the water, the sky was the limit, and people were talking about Arsenal as a major player in the transfer market, not one of the teams who just tagged on to Manchester United and Blackburn's coat tails.

As a footballer you get used to all the speculation and rumours in the papers, so when your club gets linked with the likes of Roberto Baggio and Dennis Bergkamp, you tend just to forget about it because you think the press are trying to concoct a story . Bergkamp was the name on everybody's lips because it was obvious that he was having a bad time in Italy with Inter Milan and that they wanted to off-load him. There had been a few stories linking him with Arsenal, but nothing concrete that I'd heard about.

I was at Ascot Races in the *News of the World* box when the phone rang. It was a mate of mine who couldn't hold back his excitement as he shouted: 'Arsenal have signed Dennis Bergkamp! I couldn't believe it, so I turned on the television to check Ceefax, and there it was in black and white, 'ARSENAL SIGN BERGKAMP FOR £7.5 MILLION'. I was stunned; it just didn't sink in at first. One of the greatest players in the world had joined *my* club, and I'd be playing and training alongside *Dennis Bergkamp* next season! Suddenly, I realised just how a fan must feel when he hears about a new player, that thrill, that buzz of excitement. It was brilliant.

I remembered watching him, Dennis, play for Holland and the way he destroyed England at Wembley in a friendly match a few years back with one of the best goals I have ever seen, a cushioned lob, perfectly executed, when other players would have struggled to control the ball let alone score. This was the guy who was going to be playing alongside me in an Arsenal shirt – man, what a buzz!

Signing Dennis was an inspirational move by the club and was down to Bruce and vice-chairman David Dein. The whole transfer set-up had changed at Highbury in the light of the George Graham situation and it was down to the manager to identify his targets and then put it straight into the hands of Mr Dein. As far as I'm concerned, Mr Dein was the perfect man for the job because he loves all that wheeling and dealing and is one of the shrewdest negotiators you could ever come across. He also has a brilliant knowledge of European football, knows the power-brokers and also knows what is right for Arsenal Football Club. I've known Mr Dein for years, but I think this is the most satisfied that I've ever seen him because he is playing a huge part in putting Arsenal back on the map.

Now it wasn't only the club and the fans that were buzzing, but the whole of English football. Spurs and Jürgen Klinsmann had shown that the world's best footballers did want to play in England, but we kept the ball rolling and I think that opened the door for the likes of Chelsea to sign Ruud Gullit and Newcastle to tempt David Ginola and Faustino Asprilla over to Tyneside.

But Arsenal weren't content to just sit back and say, 'Yeah, we've done the business once, let the others have a go.' Bruce was determined to get another big name in and about a month later he landed the fish he'd been after for quite a while.

David Platt's name had been bandied about as a possible target for us, but the likes of Manchester United, Blackburn and even Aston Villa seemed to be ahead of us in the race. I went on holiday with the rumours still flying around about 'Platty', but didn't think much more of them although while I was away, the rumours seemed to be getting stronger and stronger. Shortly after I got back, the club jumped into the transfer market again and splashed out £4.5 million to bring the England captain back home.

I have respect for so many players, but Platty is right up there near the top of the list. He's had his critics over the years who reckon he doesn't have the natural ability of, say, Dennis Bergkamp, but if you've ever watched Platty close up, day-in and day-out, then you'd see that the man is class.

What the hell is 'natural ability' anyway? I know thousands of people who juggle balls on their head, shoulders or backside and keep it up for a hundred times, but as long as they're breathing they'd never make a professional footballer. People say that Platty was lucky that he was in the right place at the right time to score that memorable extra-time goal for England against Belgium in their 1990 World Cup second round match. That goal might have changed his life, but I'll tell you something, luck equals preparation plus opportunity.

It wasn't luck that Platty was there when the ball came into the box; he had trained for that moment for years, timing his arrival, making space for himself and being there when it counted. And the way he scored wasn't luck either, it was a split-second of perfect technique that he'd worked for all his career. Anybody who scores as many international goals as he does isn't lucky, I should know because I've tried hard enough myself!

With Bergkamp and Platt in the side and Paul Merson back and looking good after all his problems the previous season, the football pundits really fancied us to win something. It was a feeling I definitely shared. Footballers are pretty realistic when it comes to judging their own side; we tend to know exactly what our strengths and weaknesses are and how we measure up to other teams. I looked around at the rest of the Premiership and I was pretty confident that we would be near the top of the league at the season's end.

Manchester United were always going to be challenging for honours even though they'd lost Paul Ince, Andrei Kanchelskis and Mark Hughes. After all, they still had Eric Cantona and Ryan Giggs, and 'Incey' had told me that the kids coming through were something special. Also Liverpool were going to be strong again, and I liked the look of Newcastle with their new signings.

Despite this, I thought Arsenal had what it took to be up there challenging for the championship. We had the best goalkeeper in Britain in David Seaman, our defence was always going to be tough to break down and then suddenly we had two world-class players to come into midfield and attack.

The fans obviously felt exactly the same way because before the season the expectation was higher than I'd ever known it during my time at the club. Punters would come up to me all through the summer and ask how we were going to do. When I tried to play it cool and sit on the fence, they'd say, 'No man, this is our season. We're definitely going to win something.' It was difficult not to get caught up in all the excitement and I found myself thinking about championship and cup medals before we'd even kicked a ball in pre-season training.

As soon as the players did all get together in the middle of July, I knew that the lads were all feeling exactly the same way. I always look forward to the new season, I love training with the sun on my back even if it is a slog with all the running and fitness work you have to put in during those early weeks. Then when you finally get to kick a ball around, the adrenalin comes flooding through your body and you realise just how lucky you are to be playing football for a living.

But this time there was something even more exciting, something that grabbed me and said, 'Wrighty, this is your time, you are the man this season.' Perhaps it was just the fact that I'd be playing alongside Dennis Bergkamp because from the moment I first saw him in training I knew that we were perfect for each other.

There is something in the very best players that stands out the moment they walk onto the training pitch. It's an air that they have about them, a style that singles them out from even the best of the rest, and Dennis has that. The way he runs, kicks and handles himself is special and I just had this feeling that we were going to hit it off from the start.

I'm not too proud to say that I learnt off Dennis just by watching him and seeing the positions he took up during games. He wasn't an out and out finisher like me. He has more to his game, more vision, a better passing ability and the intelligence to know exactly where players were going to be the second he received the ball. We are completely different characters but our individual games complimented each other so well. I never set myself targets before a season, but I knew with Dennis in the side I had to score at least 25 goals.

Unfortunately, the pre-season buzz didn't last too long. I don't know what it was, whether I reacted badly to a few situations or whether Bruce might have felt he handled things wrongly, but before long the manager and I were on a collision course.

It kicked off in Sweden on our pre-season tour where he and I didn't see eye-to-eye over more than a few things. It was our first time together for a long period following the close season and I think we were both feeling each other out, seeing how we got on, and finding out just what we could and couldn't say to each other. I know I'm volatile and I fly off the handle too easily, but what you see is what you get and there is no way I would cheat on my manager or team-mates either in training or match situations.

But Bruce didn't see it that way. He accused me of not putting everything into training and of not trying during some of the games in Sweden. I accepted that and tried not to react because it would have been stupid to get involved just for the sake of it. But his criticism hurt me.

Bruce also pulled me aside one day and told me that he found my language unacceptable. Now I know I don't exactly sound as if I've just stepped out of a Swiss finishing school, but I also don't swear every other word. I don't think any of the boys take offence at my language because they give as good back, it's just the usual sort of industrial banter that takes place in any office or factory. The boss, though, felt it was unnecessary and told me that I had to curb my swearing.

I could sense that there was friction between us and I should have let it go. I should have bent over backwards to get on the manager's right side, because there was no need for things to start out badly. He was just trying to get the best out of me in the way he thought was right, but I let my pride get in the way.

Instead of holding my hands up and saying, 'Yeah boss, you're right,' I let things eat away at me until they were blown out of all proportion and I'd made a major problem of them in my own mind. Psychology plays a huge part in football and in relationships between player and manager, and even though I was partly to blame with my attitude, I think that Bruce made a mistake psychologically.

I don't care if people think that I'm a prima donna, but I'm not one of those players who always reacts well to a ticking off. Sure, I can take someone tearing into me if I've done something wrong or let the team down, but the big stick approach doesn't always work. The managers who've got the best out of me know that I need an arm round my shoulder sometimes and a quiet word of encouragement every now and then.

I think during the 1995/96 season Bruce read me wrong.

He thought I was someone who reacted differently, perhaps he'd never come across someone with a similar character whom he'd had to deal with. Whatever the reasons, we got off on the wrong foot and it took a long time to get things together again.

Thankfully, I don't think there's a lasting problem between the boss and me. Over the last few months since everything came to a head with the transfer request, we've looked at each other in a different way and it's been a hell of a lot better, now I think we understand each other. You don't have to be bosom buddies with your manager, just have a mutual respect, and I feel Bruce and I now have that.

But for a while there, I'd completely and utterly lost my head. The press boys on the trip to Sweden obviously picked up on the atmosphere between me and the boss and I came home to major headlines about bust-ups and rows. It was a bit over the top, but to be honest I suppose you have to say that there was something in the stories.

On returning home to my wife Debbie, I told her how I was feeling, how I had the impression that I wasn't the manager's golden boy. As usual, she put it all in perspective, telling me that I was probably over-reacting and that I just had to get on with life and see how things went. She made it clear that I was making the problem worse than it really was, and that the boss and I had a long way to go yet.

I knew Debs was right, but the next few weeks didn't exactly help clear the air between Bruce and me. Straight after returning from Sweden, Arsenal played a friendly match against St Albans and this time the sparks really did fly.

It always happens when you come up against these non-league teams, there's always somebody who wants to make a name for themselves and tell all his mates how he put the professionals in their place. Unfortunately, I came up against the prime example. I don't even recall the player's name, all

I remember is the lumps he kicked out of me during those ninety minutes at St Albans.

I'd had a real tussle with him throughout the game, got booked for a stupid tackle and came off the pitch in a vile mood. It didn't help that Bruce tore into me virtually from the second that I sat down, accusing me of not pulling my weight, of being a big time Charlie and getting involved instead of concentrating on my game.

To this day, I can't agree with Bruce on that one. Perhaps it was his way of trying to make a psychological point, tearing into me after a game that, in the greater scheme of things, didn't really matter. I'm not a mind reader, but perhaps he was trying to make a point to the rest of the team, not just me, that he would not tolerate what he thought were falling standards, even if it was just against a bunch of part-timers.

I might have done the same in his shoes. There he was, a manager who'd never been in the top flight, put in charge of a dressing room full of internationals. He had to make an impression somehow, and had to stamp his authority on the team. He might have thought that by trying to get the best out of me his way, then it would set a precedent and people would know that he meant business. But to me, it just felt like a slap in the face. Now I've put it down to experience, but at the time it did nothing for my mood.

On reflection, perhaps I had a bit of a persecution complex, looking for shadows that weren't there, trying to read stuff into things that meant nothing. That happens when you have a new manager and you don't know where you stand, not just in football but in life. Perhaps I should have spent more time trying to get to know Bruce and to see what made him tick. Equally though, I think he could have made more of an effort with me.

Ultimately, it wasn't the situation with Bruce that led me to hand in a transfer request, although obviously that was a factor. More than anything, I stopped enjoying my football.

All players go through a stage in their careers when they feel jaded, where the day-to-day involvement becomes less enjoyable. It got to the point where I wasn't looking forward to training every morning; football was becoming a chore and not something that I loved.

To me, that was the worst feeling. Ever since the day I signed for Palace, the sheer fact that I was getting paid for kicking a ball about has never ceased to amaze me. I have always lived to train and play, to meet up with the rest of the lads every day, join in the banter and just enjoy life. But virtually from the early stages of the season, there was something in the back of my mind nagging away, telling me that this life wasn't all it's cracked up to be.

That's why I needed things to come to a head. I could have carried on – not exactly going through the motions – but playing in a sort of a bubble, doing my job but not living the life. It's not as if the goals had dried up or anything like that because I started the season on fire, everything I touched seemed to hit the back of the net and I was on a real roll.

But suddenly, goals weren't enough. The boss had introduced a new system and that was also having an effect. He wanted us to play a passing game instead of the direct style that we'd become used to in the last five or six seasons, and although the system was getting a lot of praise, all the players struggled to come to terms with it early on, especially me.

I was used to playing a certain way, the way I'd played all my career, direct and over the top where I could use my pace to its full extent. It's the way that Palace had played and certainly the way George Graham had us playing, and to suddenly adapt after nine or ten years came as a bit of a culture shock.

I have always played in a partnership, whether it was with Mark Bright at Palace or Alan Smith or Kevin Campbell at Arsenal. I had never before played as a lone striker. But here I was, up front on my own for the first time and I was struggling to come to terms with it. As I said earlier, Dennis is not the sort of forward who plays in the front-line, he drops back into the space, picks up loose balls and suddenly springs us into attack. That meant I was the only target whenever the defence or midfield wanted to ease the pressure and I was having to adapt to a completely different strategy.

I'll never complain about having to work hard, but I found myself chasing around like a blue-arsed fly trying to cover the width of the pitch. So many times the ball would be played exactly where I like it, but I'd find myself on the wrong side of the pitch and too knackered to even make a move for it, let alone get there in front of the defender.

Just to make matters worse, as a team we weren't playing very well. We were getting the odd result here and there, but we just didn't seem capable of putting a decent run together that would lift us up with the leaders. The major problem was our lack of consistency. We'd pick up a couple of wins and feel that we were about to really get going, then we'd go and draw the next two or draw one and lose one. It was that kind of season, certainly up to Christmas.

It took a long time for it to dawn on us that we were in a transitional period and really we shouldn't have expected to romp away with the league in our first season under a new manager playing a completely different system. But we were guilty of getting carried away with our own publicity and with the expectations of the fans; we were lulled into a false sense of confidence when really we should have been working harder to get things right.

Slowly, I felt the frustration building up within me. I knew what we had to do – all the players knew – but we just weren't able to get it right. That was leading to rows in the dressing room and I felt I was being singled out for most of the criticism. Perhaps it was the general mood that I was in, but I felt some of the things were unfair and that I was being made a scapegoat.

Things reached a head in the dressing room in January during the FA Cup Third Round match with Sheffield United. We hadn't played particularly well, in fact we'd been absolutely diabolical against a team we should have swatted aside without a second thought. The boss slaughtered us at half-time, particularly John Hartson and myself, and although we hadn't set the world alight, we were no worse than anybody else. I scored in the second half but United equalised just before the end and could even have nicked it with a couple of minutes to go. As we came in, I knew the boss was about to explode but even I wasn't ready for the volley aimed in my direction. He gave it everything, saying that I was lazy, big time, that I wasn't pulling my weight, and even criticised me for sometimes not eating my food when we went away to hotels!

I can look back and laugh at it now and realise that a lot of it was said in the heat of the moment. Bruce was obviously gutted that we had played so badly and at times like that you sometimes say things either you don't mean or that have no relevance to the situation. I should know, I've done it enough times myself. But at the time, the criticism hurt me and I reacted badly, giving Bruce a mouthful back.

Again, on reflection, we were both in the wrong. Some of what Bruce said to me was a bit over the top, but I don't suppose I helped by giving him some back. Whatever the rights or wrongs, I think the rest of the lads were stunned at just how bad things had got between me and the boss. Tony Adams pulled me up and just said, 'Wrighty, you've got to get that sorted out quickly.' I should have listened to Tony. I should have made the first move and been big enough to go to Bruce and get things cleared up.

Instead, I let my anger and pride get in the way again. I was determined not to be the one to back down, I felt that I was justified in the way I reacted, and it was better to get things out in the open so that the lads knew exactly how I felt.

Just to pile on more grief, people were coming out of the woodwork with even more rubbish about me. I know I've got a reputation that makes me an easy target, but some of the lies being spread around were absolutely unforgivable. First of all, Roger Nilssen, the Sheffield United defender, claimed in an article for some foreign newspaper that I'd spat at him during the FA Cup match at Highbury. The papers over here picked it up and just a few days before we had to go to Bramall Lane for the replay, there's a 'Wright Spit Hate' story splashed all across the back pages.

Let's get it right, now. I didn't spit at Nilssen, he knew it was just a way to wind me up before a big game and, give him his due, it worked like a dream. I was rubbish in the replay and United beat us 1–0 and that was that, out of the Cup at the first attempt. The only consolation was that several of the United players came up and said, 'Sorry for what Nilssen did, it was bang out of order and we know you didn't spit at him, he was just trying to stir it.' Even though we lost, that meant something to me.

But once you get a bad report, it sticks and just a week later, I was accused of spitting again, this time at a little girl when we played at Middlesborough. It was so pathetic that I had to laugh. Some woman rang a newspaper and told them that I'd spat on her little grand-daughter during the match at the Riverside Stadium, so the paper trotted out this picture of a lovely little girl looking angelic and quoted her as say, 'Why did he do that granny? It wasn't very nice.'

No way, man, I certainly didn't spit at the girl, her granny or any other Middlesborough fan that day. Several eye-witnesses verified that I didn't go within 25 yards of that part of the stand all day, so how the hell could I have soaked this little girl with spit?. These are the same Middlesborough fans who reported Alan Shearer to the police for celebrating a Blackburn goal, claiming it was incitement to riot. If they were so outraged at an opposition striker clenching his fist after he scored, don't you think that they'd be beating the police station door down if I'd even thought about spitting? As it was, there was not one complaint to the police and the whole sad little incident disappeared after a few days, but it was enough to make me wonder if it was all worthwhile.

Suddenly, I had this feeling that everything was closing in on me, that there was this extra pressure that I had never experienced before. Things weren't going right on the pitch, off the pitch I wasn't having the best of times and even outside football the same old garbage was going down. I battled on for as long as I could, but I knew eventually something had to give.

Throughout this period, the thought constantly nagged at the back of my mind, 'Do I have to leave Arsenal?' The more I thought about it, the more I realised that getting away from Highbury was the only solution – or so it seemed at the time. I convinced myself that I was cheating the club and the fans because my mind wasn't right, I wasn't 100 per cent focused and I was letting myself down. I spoke about it with Debs, and even though she was shocked at just how far I was willing to go, she backed me to the hilt.

Then it was a case of asking advice from those people whom I trusted. I went to my agent, Jerome Anderson, whom I first met back in May 1988. I had been selected to play for a Football League XI, whose keeper that day was Tony Coton, and he had asked Jeff Weston from his agents Jerome Anderson Management to accompany him. I put in a good performance, and after the game Jeff collared Tony and asked him for an introduction. I had a chat and arranged to meet Jeff and Jerome Anderson a week later, at which point I agreed to join them. At that stage, when agents were mentioned, you just thought of people ripping you off and that you had to be wary, but in this case I knew I could trust them. Throughout my playing career, Jerome has never once given me a bad piece of advice. He's an Arsenal nut but he's also got only my best interests at heart, and although he was just as surprised as Debs had been at my wanting to leave Arsenal, he promised to do everything he could to help me.

We talked about it for hours, discussing all the different possibilities and whether a transfer request was the right thing or whether I should sit it out until the end of the season and bite the bullet in the hope that things might turn around. I couldn't see how that might happen, but it was a consideration I had to take, so I backed off from slapping in a request.

When I eventually did put it in writing, there was a lot written in the papers about how this was a ploy by me to force Bruce Rioch out of Arsenal. That's complete and utter rubbish. It may sound selfish, but all I was interested in was doing the right thing for myself and then the club; I wasn't interested in how it might effect some supposed power battle within the boardroom.

At the time, Bruce still hadn't signed a contract despite being at the club for nine months or so. There was some suggestion that he and David Dein weren't getting along, that the boss wanted more say in transfers and Mr Dein was having too much influence within the dressing room. People automatically assumed that just because me and Mr Dein are close friends, it must have been some sort of plan cooked up between us to push Bruce out the door once the fans started protesting over my transfer.

I'd be kidding myself if I thought I was such an important part of the Highbury jigsaw. I've seen how fans react when a player, even a popular player, gets sold. For a couple of weeks they're up in arms, moaning about how it's a disgrace and a disaster that the club are letting their best players go. Then as soon as a replacement is found, the former player is forgotten. By the time he comes back with his new team, he's a Judas and gets roasted every time he gets the ball!

There was no thought in my mind about throwing down

an ultimatum to anybody. I know that nobody at Arsenal is bigger than the club and that goes for the players, the managers and even the directors. Arsenal are one of the greatest clubs in the world with an amazing history, and anybody arrogant enough to believe that he is suddenly more important deserves to be booted out of Highbury.

The day I decided to hand in my request was one of the hardest of my life. I sat down with Jerome and decided carefully what to write, because there was no way that I wanted to wind anybody up, I just wanted to put down clearly what I thought and believed. I honestly felt that it would be in the club's interest for me to leave and make a fresh start somewhere else.

I had enough faith in my ability to know that other clubs would be interested once it became common knowledge that I wanted to leave Arsenal, but I also knew in my heart that anything else would be second best to Highbury. That was a risk I was willing to take just to get my mind and career back on track.

I handed the letter personally to Bruce at the training ground and also sent a copy to Mr Dein and the chairman, Peter Hill-Wood. Although he knew that I wasn't happy, I think Bruce was shocked and upset that I'd decided to go that far and make things official. He called me into his office and we sat down and had a quick chat. He told me straight away that he didn't want me to go, and that he would recommend to the board that they turn down the request. That was nice to hear, but at the time it didn't make any difference to the way I felt. The board could turn it down, but I still wanted to get away.

Mr Dein and Mr Hill-Wood also got in touch with me to say how upset they were to hear about my decision and asked me to change my mind. I think it was a bit of an eye-opener for the chairman, he doesn't keep in close contact with the players and to hear that somebody was that unhappy came as a shock to him. They both said that they didn't think the board would back the request, but again I felt as if I had to carry it through.

The week before I handed the request in, the Sunday newspapers had linked me with Chelsea and although I'd had no contact with either Glenn Hoddle or anybody from the Chelsea board, it started things off in my mind. They were playing some great stuff last season; Hoddle was one of my idols and it would be brilliant to link up with the likes of Ruud Gullit, Dennis Wise and Mark Hughes. The club obviously had big plans despite the fact that there was all that trouble between Ken Bates and Matthew Harding.

I met Harding in a West End restaurant a few days later when I was with some friends and he was out with a chairman from another club. It was so embarrassing because it looked like such a set-up, and I was worried that if word got back to Arsenal, then major questions would be raised. I knew that I had to do things properly and there was no way I was going behind Arsenal's back to try and engineer a move. If it happened, great. If not, then I'd be glad to stay at Highbury as long as I got a few things sorted out.

If I'm totally honest, I felt for a lot of the season that I was being taken for granted so when I put the request in and other clubs started sniffing around, it was nice to have my ego boosted. Chelsea were definitely interested, and I know that Harry Redknapp would have had me at West Ham given the slightest bit of encouragement.

For three or four days after the news leaked out, everything went mental. The phone didn't stop ringing, everywhere I went people stopped me to find out exactly what was happening and the papers were filled with stories about where I was going, who Arsenal were getting in to replace me and the so-called 'war' I was having with the boss.

The Arsenal fans were magnificent. Sure, I got letters from a few idiots telling me to get lost and good riddance, but most of the mail I received was very supportive. Punters were writing to say that they would be sorry to see me go, but wished me well and thanked me for everything that I had done for the club. That lifted me, knowing that the guys who pay their money every week appreciated my efforts and wouldn't hold it against me if I did leave.

In the end, it was all academic. There was a board meeting at which Bruce recommended that the transfer request be knocked on the head, the directors agreed and that was that, I wasn't leaving Arsenal at any price. When I heard the decision, I had to admit I wasn't really surprised, and in a way it lifted the clouds that had been hanging over me for most of the season. I wasn't sure if it was right for me to stay, but when the most powerful people at a club say that they want you to stay and that you're an important part of their future plans, then you have to hold your hands up and say, 'Hey, I'm honoured that you value me so highly.'

Bruce made it clear that we would have to talk and try and sort out the problems that were obviously getting me down. He went up a few notches in my mind then, because it would have been easy for him just to snub me and let me get on with the rest of the season. I think it was then that I realised what a tough job he had on his hands, coming in cold to a club that had the stuffing kicked out of it the previous year and trying to rebuild it both on and off the pitch.

Now Bruce and I are never going to be bosom buddies. We're not exactly going to be round each other's house every other night, laughing and joking and having a beer. But there is a mutual respect between us now that may have taken some time to build, but I think it will be there for quite a while. I can see things from his viewpoint and I'm sure he realises where I'm coming from now. There will be times when we clash, but I've clashed with Steve Coppell and George Graham and I'll clash with any manager, that's just the way I am. I play from the heart and if things aren't going right, then I'm not the sort to go sit quietly in a corner, I react passionately.

The boss shares that passion, even if we're not coming from the same angle on it. He cares deeply for the game, and I'm sure he cares just as deeply for Arsenal as I do and that's the only thing that counts.

There were stories doing the rounds last season that he told me in training how John McGinlay used to finish at Bolton and compared me unfavourably with him. That's nonsense. We did used to talk about other strikers and their style and technique but he never once tried to get me to be another John McGinlay. I think he had far too much respect for me and my record as a goal-scorer to ever get me to change.

I can honestly say that we have cleared the air now. The boss gave me assurances about the future, that I wasn't about to be cast aside in some major rebuilding plan and that he valued me highly as a player. In return, I told him honestly that I never, ever wanted to leave Arsenal and it would have broken my heart to quit Highbury, but at the time I felt it was the only option open to me.

The last few weeks of the season went by in a bit of a blur. We only ever played to our true form six or seven times in the season but were still able to get a place in Europe after we finished fifth. To be fair to the boss and the players, fifth was just about right because we never showed the sort of consistency that Villa, Liverpool, Newcastle and Manchester United all achieved. You have to be realistic about these things, and I'm sure the boys will back me up when I say that only the games against Leeds, Everton and Southampton in the league and Newcastle in the Coca-Cola Cup stand out as top-notch team performances by the Gunners.

We know that we have to set higher standards this season, especially if we're going to do anything in Europe, but that's the thing driving me on now. I've seen close up what players like Dennis Bergkamp bring to even the best of clubs and if we get in a few more of his quality, then we will be one hell of a side. Possibly the league will have to wait another year, but you never know. Alex Ferguson tore a side apart and went on to pick up the Double, so there's hope for all of us.

As for me, I still feel I've got at least four good years left in me playing at the very top. I'm contracted to Arsenal until then 1999, hand on heart, I never want to leave. Last season was the blip on my screen, even though I did score 25 goals, and I never want to go through something like that again. I'm sure I've got it out of my system and now I'm looking forward to the rest of my career at the best club in Britain.

2
In and Out
of School

Football has always been in my blood, right from the moment my brother Morris told me how he would always be better than me at everything! Just trying to compete and be better than him drove me on, even when I was just a little kid who could hardly stand up, let alone kick a ball.

There were four of us: my eldest brother, Nicky, who is three years older than me; Morris, who's a year or so older; then me; and finally my baby sister Dionne. Our real family name is Maclean, but my dad, Herbert, left when I was about four, so we took our mum, Nesta's, maiden name. I don't blame my dad for walking out, and I can't say that I really missed him. He would come round now and again and we'd get on, just like I get on with him now when I see him, so I don't have any big hang-ups about him not being around. My step-dad, Winston, was always on the scene, so I didn't miss that father-figure presence.

But it was my mum who was the driving force behind our family. I don't know how she did it at times, but there was always food on the table and we always had decent clothes, which wasn't always the case with families in our part of south London.

I was born in the Woolwich Military hospital on 3 November 1963, and from the moment I was born it seemed that we were always moving house. Deptford, Brockley, Peckham, Lewisham, Crofton Park: you name a part of south-east London and I guarantee I've lived there at some time or another. And it wasn't just the four of us under one roof with my mum. When I was 10, my three girl cousins, Margaret, Pamela and Paulette, came to live with us until they emigrated to America. With seven kids in the house, it must have driven my mum crazy, especially the time when she came back from bingo to find that Pamela had nearly burnt the house down after cooking fried dumplings and the pan caught light!

My mum seemed to just deal with it and take it all in her stride, except when I would come home with my best shoes smashed to bits through playing football. My trainers would last about two minutes before being busted up from kicking about in the street or school playground. So I'd wear my best shoes, and my mum would just go mad that they were ruined. Morris always made his trainers last, so when it came to getting a new pair, he would lend me his old ones to play football in. But then we'd have a monster row and he'd just say 'Get my trainers off' and I'd be right back where I started, busting up every pair of shoes I had!

It was really Morris who inspired me to become good at football – just so I could shut him up! Believe me, he was the world's best at winding me up when it came to football. Nicky was quick and a good tackler, but Morris was far more naturally gifted than either of us and he would always let us know it. He didn't give Nicky too much lip, otherwise he would get battered, but I always came in for loads of grief.

I was jealous of Morris because he'd continually tease me about not having a hard shot or being able to kick with my left foot or being able to head a ball properly. I didn't realise it then, but he drove me to practise with my left foot because I so wanted to be better than him at everything. I look back now and think that, if it hadn't been for Morris winding up his little brother, then I might not have had the drive and determination to become a footballer. He was horrible when we were kids, but now my left foot is just as good as my right – although I'm still not that good in the air!

It wasn't just football, though: I always wanted to beat Morris at anything. If we were going out with Mum, he said he was dressed better than me. If we were going to school, then he'd say his shoes or his bag looked better than mine: it riled me so much, you wouldn't believe it! But when Morris, Nicky , I and three of our mates got together in a team, we were virtually unbeatable. We would go over to the local park and ask other groups of kids if they wanted a game, and we almost always won. I was always up front, on the left wing and involved in scoring goals: it just came naturally, even then. Morris and I would have our West Ham shirts on – him with 10 on the back, me with 8 – and we would just hammer the other kids. I think Morris could have been a player himself, but just wasn't bothered and kind of drifted away from football.

My first organised game was when I was eight and at Gordon Brock Junior School. I can still remember it because the teacher, Mr King, had to lend me a pair of boots and they were too big. They were the old George Best ones with the little white flash and I thought I was the business. We lost 3–2 to Fairlawn, but I scored and I suppose you can say that's where it all started.

It was also the start of my disciplinary problems. Even at that age I would go mental if we were losing or things weren't going right for me, and it was usually my team-mates who got slaughtered. I'd tell them to f*** off, or to get their f***ing fingers out, it was nasty but I couldn't stop myself because I wanted to win so badly. If we lost, then I'd really go wild, I'd cry and want to fight people. Most of the Arsenal players will tell you that nothing's changed, I've just got bigger and nastier! I'm so embarrassed when I look back on it, because I must have the been the most horrible little brat around. I can still remember one five-a-side competition that my side won, where I was swearing at the referee, at my team-mates, at the opposition and even the people watching. I even cried and ranted and raved on the pitch when the other team scored. Afterwards, one of the players came up to me and told me that if I had been twenty years older, his dad would have knocked me out. To be fair, I would have deserved it.

It wasn't until I started my secondary school, Samuel Pepys in Brockley, that a couple of teachers got hold of me and started to straighten me out a bit. Mr Melborn used to show me that I couldn't go around swearing and slaughtering people or getting into tantrums because things weren't going right. He told me I thought I was God's gift to football and that I ought to come down to earth, and he made sure that happened. If he was refereeing a game, I knew I was going to get sent off. He'd disallow a perfectly good goal for offside, and if I dared say anything, that would be it, straight off. If I ever sulked, you could guarantee I wouldn't last long on the pitch, and slowly I began to control my emotions. Mr McCarthy also used to keep me in check. He would never shout at me or really tell me off, but I was a bit scared of him and I respected him, so he could just say something quietly and put the fear of God into me. Between those two, they put me on the right path.

But if my football was beginning to get straightened out, I was still a nightmare in the classroom. The area where I'm from is rough and you had to be a bit streetwise, especially when people were pouring out of the pubs every night look-ing for fights or just to mess you around. I got a bit of respect because people knew I was good at football and they knew I had a couple of brothers who could look after themselves, and me, if it came to a fight. But I still took that street attitude into the classroom. I had to be the one always at the centre of attention, making people laugh and disrupting the classes. It would be silly things like pulling chairs away when people were going to sit down, but it also got more serious.

I would get caned for swearing at the teachers, smoking in the toilets and playing truant, everything like that. I don't really know why I did it, because the headmaster, Mr Cleal, frightened the life out of me. He was so strict, the typical sergeant-major-looking man with the big moustache, a nice three-piece suit and his gold watch chain, and, man, I used to cry when he caned me.

My reports always said the same: Ian could do well, but he just doesn't seem to want to try, and they were right. I was intelligent, in all the top classes throughout my secondary school, but all I wanted to do was muck around and be the clown who everybody liked and laughed with. The teachers always told me that I'd regret it, regret not taking care of my education, and even now that I've done all right out of football, I still wish I'd worked harder at school.

Thankfully, I think the teachers liked me, because they never gave up on me. At Samuel Pepys, I was suspended for overstepping the mark just once too often, and when I came back they put me in a special class called 'The Unit' where the disruptive kids were lumped together. That was where I finally got my act together because I knew that I had reached the end of the road, and if I went out of line again, I was in deep, deep trouble.

Football was the one thing that was keeping me in school. If I hadn't had that, then I would have been out of there, big time, and on the street. But even football had a way of kicking me in the teeth. I played for the school and my district, Blackheath, all the way through, but when it came to playing for Inner London, then I got knocked back. I can still remember it to this day, travelling across south London to Raynes Park for Inner London trials and the teacher, Mr Silverman, just telling me I wasn't good enough, no reason, nothing, just go. I cried for every second of that journey home.

I also learnt a few good lessons as well. I wasn't flash because that's the biggest crime you can commit in the area I'm from, but I've always been cocky on and off the football pitch. One day, I found out that I had pushed it too far when one of my own team-mates punched me in the face and gave me the biggest black eye you've ever seen, after we'd had an argument on the pitch. The same thing happened a few years later when I'd left school and was playing for my Sunday team, Ten Em Bee. I was good, and everybody knew how good I was, so I was giving it the big 'un in training when one of my team-mates tackled me. I got straight up and said, 'You f***ing idiot, what are you tackling me like that for?' and that was it, BANG! The geezer gave me a massive head-butt, right on my nose and there was blood everywhere. I didn't say anything, I just took it and realised I had to keep a few things to myself. I'm sure there were a few people at the time who thought, 'Yeah, serves him right,' and it did serve me right, but it also taught me not to get too flash and big-headed about things.

Even now, sometimes I don't like myself for some of the things I say and do on the pitch. Other players know that I talk on the pitch. I try to wind the opposition up, to get myself going, and most players take it as part and parcel of the game, but even then I'll go too far. Arsenal played against Hartlepool a couple of seasons ago and I was determined not to speak to the guy who was marking me. Lower division players always want you to bite when they give you tons of mouth or kick you from here to next week, and if you do go down from a challenge, it's always, 'Get up, you big-time Charlie,' so I was determined not to crack. I was talking to Paul Merson when the ball had run out of play, but this guy was continually in my ear, so I snapped and turned to him and said, 'Piss off. I don't talk to Third Division players.'

That shocked me and it shocked him because it wasn't a nice thing to say, but sometimes I just can't help myself. I know I can never change; I just hope people don't always think too badly of me.

I've always given referees stick, and sometimes I've gone too far, but some officials are just as bad. We were playing in a pre-season friendly against Southend last summer and I got involved in a bad tackle with one of their lads. Now I knew it was a dodgy challenge and I held my hands up, but the referee had a point to make and he said, 'I see your attitude hasn't changed.' That was unnecessary, and I know I shouldn't have done a thing, but I said, 'No, but my wages have.' That's just as stupid, but I felt I needed to say it at the time. Yet afterwards I thought how dumb it must have sounded and I was embarrassed. Throughout my life, I've always been caught up in the emotion of the game, and those one-liners come flying out. I'd like to be able to stop it, but sometimes my mouth runs away with me.

That competitive edge got me into fights at school, even at primary school. There's always that myth when you're kids that the best footballer is always supposed to be the best fighter. It's stupid, but I know it's the same all over the country because I've talked to other players who found themselves in the same situation. So there I was, one of the best footballers in the school and supposed to be one of the top fighters (even though nobody ever knew why!) and a kid called Paul Smith wanted to prove himself against me. We were playing a game one day and suddenly everybody was ganging up to see us have a go at each other. It must have been the longest fight on record! We started at dinner time, carried it on after school and then came back the next morning and carried on where we'd left off: I just couldn't believe what was going on. In the end, nobody knew who won, it just petered out and we started life again.

But trouble seemed to follow me wherever I went. At

Samuel Pepys I had a bit of a way and a strut, and guys always wanted to have a piece of me. By then I was on The Unit and anybody in there was considered to be a nutcase, so by and large I got left alone, except for one bloke who was mouthing off at me all the time. We met face-to-face in a corridor one time and I knew something was going to happen, but just as I was tensing up he said, 'Just because you've got all your mates with you.' I looked round and whereas two seconds before I had been on my own, now it was as if the whole school had incredibly appeared from nowhere to watch this showdown! I'm telling you, it was madness, man.

In between fights, suspensions and canings, I was at least managing to make a name for myself in sport. At infants school I'd been captain of the mixed rounders team. I always loved cricket, and I was in the second five for basketball, but it was always football that was number one in my heart. I was all raw ability. I didn't appreciate other players around me and I'd never pass the ball to anybody. It wasn't until I was about 12 that I began to realise that I had to pass to other players sometimes, that the game wasn't just about me as an individual trying to beat thirty men and scoring a goal. Even playing for my school and my district, Blackheath, I was the same: going for glory when I should have been setting others up.

Perhaps that was part of the reason why professional clubs weren't too interested. Most of the other boys in the Blackheath side were linking up with clubs: one would be going to Charlton, another to Millwall, so-and-so to Crystal Palace or QPR, and there was me, Ian Wright, going absolutely nowhere. Also I don't think my face really fitted on the professional scene at the time – I had a look, and the way I talked and acted must have put some of them off, without a doubt. I was also pretty small for my age and I tried to kid myself that was the reason why nobody was interested, but Andy Gray, who I'd link up again with at Palace later in life, was the same size and he was getting through all these trials, so I was gutted.

The only sniff that I ever had was with Millwall. I was 14 at the time and they were the local team to me and the side I used to worship. A mate and I would bunk in at the old Den at the Cold Blow Lane End to watch the Lions, so it was a dream come true when they invited me to the Crofton Leisure Centre for a six-week trial. I know I showed enough in skill and ability in that time to warrant something from it; instead I got nothing, and that began a love-hate affair with Millwall that lasts even until today.

The one thing I do remember vividly was training with Keith 'Rhino' Stevens, who has been Mr Millwall for about a million years, with a reputation for eating strikers and not worrying about where he throws the bones. But I'll tell you what, he was a lot nicer in those days! A kid called David Pope smashed into him one day, knocked him over and then kicked him, and all Rhino did was pick himself up and get on with the game. Six months later he was making his debut in the first team and the crowd had turned him into a psychopath!

That was when my dream of being a footballer started to fade. When I was younger I thought, 'Yeah, man, no sweat, I'm good enough to be a pro.' But as time went on and all the other boys started to get picked up by clubs, I thought that was it, the end of the road. I didn't know about clubs taking players in their twenties without an apprenticeship or anything like that.

The geezer who got rid of me at Millwall was Roger Cross, who's now the assistant manager at Spurs. And he did it badly, with no feeling or thought for what it might be doing to a young kid. It was just, 'Leave your name and address, son, we might be in touch', when they knew full well they were never going to see you again as long as you lived. Well, Roger was wrong, and it gave me great satisfaction when he came up to me last season and asked for my autograph for a couple of kids.

One thing that did keep me going, and has always been with me in whatever I have done, was a faith in God. I don't go shouting about it and I'm not some kind of Born Again Christian, but religion has always played a major part in my life. My mum used to make us all go to church on a Sunday, but in those days when I was a kid, that Christian Baptist church used to play strange tricks on me. No matter how much I'd eaten before we left, I was always starving hungry as soon as I got there. Perhaps it was the wooden pews or the hymns, but all I could think of was sweets and what I was going to spend my collection money on as soon as I got out of church. Some of the biggest rows I ever had with my brothers were about whether we would buy a Mars Bar or a Galaxy on our way home. To me, God and religion meant chocolate for many years!

Mum knew what was going on, and in the end she used to give us just enough money to make a noise in the bottom of the bag and that was it, nothing for sweets. That was when the priest's words began to sink in. What you have to remember is that no matter how much you're not paying attention, something will always sink in. It doesn't matter whether you're talking to drunks, tramps, anybody – there is always some kind of sense in what they say.

I fear God because He's powerful and jealous and, if you don't do the right thing, then He'll smite you, man. That's the philosophy that I always go by, but He's also inspiring. I believe that if you try your hardest and if you believe in Him, then there's no way you can fail. If you don't have faith in Him, then you will have to answer to Him, no doubt about it. When I do eventually meet God, I'll try and reason with Him, tell Him I was misunderstood while I was down here, because nobody wants to go to Hell.

So there I was, a kid with all the faith and ambition in the world as well as the belief in my own talent, but with nowhere to go in professional football. I'd given up on school a year before I was supposed to leave; I hadn't done a scrap of work or revision for any exams, and anyway, I knew I wasn't going to stick around to take them. For me, it was just a case of getting out of Samuel Pepys as quick as I could to get a bit of money in my pocket and play football for local sides at the weekend.

3
Wright and Wrong

I left school at 16 with nothing, not a bit of paper to my name or any kind of skill except how to kick a ball about, and that didn't seem to be doing me much good as far as a career was concerned. All I knew was that I wanted to get a few quid in my pocket as quickly as possible. I didn't want to steal money because it would have broken my mum's heart. Her generation are so scared of the police or a police car coming to the house, that if I had got into any serious trouble at all, the shame of it would have killed her. Little did I know that within four years I would be serving a prison sentence.

My first brush with crime came when I got my first job, and all my good intentions nearly went out of the window. It was a good, decent job in a sports shop, and it was something that I wanted to do because it still meant there was some kind of link-up with sport and it brought in a nice bit of cash. I'd been unemployed for about six months after leaving Samuel Pepys, so I was pleased to have this job. But in the first week a load of my mates from our estate came round for just one thing – to nick a load of gear. It was so obvious. I knew what was going on and I just said, 'Listen, I ain't gonna stop you thieving anything, but if you get caught, don't get me involved.'

Sure enough, a guy called Trevor swiped some Wrangler

cords but got caught on the way out. He kept his mouth shut, but the bloke in charge of the shop said that I was supposed to be watching and, if I didn't stop them, then I must have been involved as well, and I was sacked from my first job, just like that. The police were called in and came round to my house to see if there was any stolen stuff from the shop there. I hadn't nicked anything so they went away happy, but even more of a relief was the fact that my mum wasn't in on the day they came round, so she was spared the sight of them knocking on her door. I think that was the day that I discovered there really IS a God, because if my mum had been there, I swear I would have been beaten from here to next week. Even now she hits me and my brothers if we step out of line, so you can just imagine how bad it would have been at 16!

I was knocking round with a group of blokes who were four or five years older than me which led to loads of bother. I know now that I should have stuck with kids my own age, playing football or snooker, but I had to be Mr Big Time and knock around with guys who were into serious stuff, not just nicking the odd bar of chocolate. I won't name names because it was too long ago, but a couple of those guys gave me the fright of my life. We were just walking past a row of shops when suddenly we ducked into a jeweller's. Perhaps I was too young to realise what was going on, but before long my eyes were wide open! One of the guys just reached over and grabbed a tray of rings, and without a second thought legged it out of the shop and down the road faster than Ben Johnson on speed. The other guy followed him, realised that I was frozen to the spot and just screamed 'Run!' I didn't need a second invitation and I was off like a shot, down the road just legging it on sheer adrenalin and fear, scared to death that the shop owner or the police would be right behind me. We got away, but suddenly I realised that this was the big league and I was getting dragged into it.

But if I got off lightly then, there was worse to come about a year later. One of Morris's friends wanted to break into a hi-fi shop in Brockley to steal some speakers for his car or something. Morris went along to help him, and I and my mate Richard were acting as look-outs from the roof of a row of shops. Somebody must have seen us on the roof, called the police and, within a few minutes, the old Bill came roaring up, lights flashing and sirens screaming. Morris and the other guy got away, but they nicked Richard and me and took us down to the local station.

We didn't have any tools or anything like that on us, so the police kept asking what the hell we were doing up on the roof. I just told them that we weren't doing anything and we were just up on the roof for a laugh, for something to do. The police didn't believe me, so not to make it so bad on myself I told them I was going to break into the greengrocer's next door to the hi-fi shop so I could get some food for my family.

Little did I know that Richard was spinning a different yarn and said we were planning to break into the jeweller's, two shops down! That was it, the police had something, but because our stories didn't match in any way apart from the fact we were on the roof together, we both got charged with vagrancy!

We went to court and were sitting there waiting to go before the magistrate when two of the scruffiest lawyers in the world – probably working for Legal Aid – came up to us in utter amazement and asked if we wanted help because they only ever saw tramps and down-and-outs charged with vagrancy, and that was only if they'd been living on the streets for a long time. I don't know whether they did any good for me, but I got 76 hours' community service in Brockley, painting and gardening. The thing that judges or magistrates don't realise is that you meet some of the nastiest villains in the world doing community service. If you wanted to go down that path, it would be so easy to pick up a good few tips while you're weeding some old lady's garden.

But that was small time compared to the next bother I found myself in, bother that would straighten me out within a week. It was when I'd first got into cars just after my 17th birthday and I had two motors: a Vauxhall Viva which I'd picked up for £60 and a Fiat 124 Special which was brown and beige with Wolf race wheels, and I thought I was the bee's knees. I had no tax, no insurance and no MOT, and I swear I used to get stopped every other day just driving around south London. I'd end up in court, get fined, but wouldn't bother paying anything. In fact I never even used to turn up when I was due to pay any money. If the police came round, then my brothers would say they didn't know where I was, and for a couple of nights I'd stay with mates until the heat wore off.

This must have gone on for about six months, but then I got a labouring job and I had a couple of quid in my pocket so I decided to be the honest citizen and start paying my fines off. So I trotted down to the Camberwell Magistrates Court and told them that I was willing to pay a fiver a month until the fines were cleared. They checked my record and asked if I would mind just waiting for a moment. I said, 'Sure, no sweat,' but five minutes later two policemen arrived, arrested me for non-payment of fines and I found myself in the cells at Camberwell Police Station. A day later I was doing five days in Chelmsford Prison!

I can't describe what those five days were like, except to say they scared the hell out of me, make no mistake. I looked at my life and I realised just what sort of mistakes I was making, and they were big mistakes. I can't say that if it wasn't for football, then I would be doing a prison sentence now, because I pray that wouldn't be the case, but the life I was leading was doing me no favours at all. Driving round south London in cars with no tax, insurance or MOT, flitting in and out of jobs, doing community service: it doesn't take a genius to work out that I wasn't exactly heading anywhere.

That's why I consider myself lucky to have done time in Chelmsford, even though that sounds stupid. It was as if God was making me dip my toes and then saying, 'Wrighty, is this how you want to spend the rest of your days?' I knew the answer to that one because I was scared stiff from first thing in the morning to last thing at night. Now, when I drive around in an expensive car or look at the big house that I live in, I know just how lucky I was to have learned a huge lesson so early on. Don't ever be fooled by films that make prison life out to be anything less than the worst experience in the world, because, believe me, it is hell on earth. I shared a cell with a huge geezer from the East End whom I was too scared of even to ask what he had done, but he took me under his wing and taught me how to make the bed properly and the basic rules of prison.

But he didn't prepare me for the hardest lesson I had to learn during my time in Chelmsford. I was lying on my bed on the second day of my sentence when a prison officer came into our cell. That was it, my cell-mate was up and standing to attention, but I just lay there with my hands behind my head wondering what was going on.

I said to the screw, 'Listen, I'm only in for five days for non-payment of fines, what day will I actually be released?'

Before I knew it, the screw had grabbed me by my throat and literally thrown me up against a wall. 'You won't be going f***ing anywhere with an attitude like that, you little s***,' he screamed at me. 'Now get up, make that bed properly and stand up when I come into your cell.'

That was it, from then on I was a nervous wreck. The cocky little teenage Jack-the-Lad had gone, and I just wanted to get through this nightmare with my nose clean and my body in one piece. I'd seen all the Jimmy Cagney films where the prisoners march round some exercise yard, but I couldn't believe it actually happened until I had to do it for the first time. All these men with nothing to do but walk round in circles: I tell you, man, it just did my head in, and I realised right there and then that this wasn't the life for me.

On the last night in Chelmsford, they put me on the wing with all the sex cases and the 'nonces', and that was the final straw. I was so afraid, I couldn't sleep a wink, and that convinced me that this life wasn't for me, plus the fact that I never want to smoke Old Holborn roll-ups ever again...!

I'd fallen foul of the law and I'm thankful that it frightened me so badly that I never, ever wanted to do anything that would put me back in prison. Those five days were like five years to me, especially on the days when I was banged up for 24 hours. That almost killed me. I realised then that I couldn't face prison or a life as a small-time crook or whatever, and that I had to do something positive. Even if I hadn't been a footballer, I think I would have lived a positive life away from the kind of influences that were threatening to drag me down.

Sometimes when I'm at training, and I'm showing off, I catch myself and think back to those days in prison and realise I shouldn't be too cocky, because just around the corner is a life that I never want to lead again.

I was also having problems with my private life. I'd moved in with a girl called Sharon only about a year after leaving school. She already had a son, Shaun, who I treated as if he was my own and who still has my name. I don't think that we were ever going to get married, and by the time I was 20, the relationship was coming to an end and we both knew that it was inevitable that I would move out. But just as the day was fast approaching when I knew I had to go, for both our sakes, Sharon found out she was pregnant with my second son, Bradley. It wasn't Sharon's fault, but I felt trapped, and I knew that there was no way we could spend the rest of our lives together. Eventually I did move out and started seeing another girl. Again, I knew that this was another relationship that wasn't going to be the long-term love of my life, and again I began to get itchy feet. But it was just like history repeating itself because the girl fell pregnant and I soon had a third son, Brett.

I know when people read this, they're going to think, 'Christ, he's put it about a bit', and in a way they're right. But I love my kids dearly and if I've ever hurt them in any way, then it has never been on purpose and I hope they can forgive me for not always being around when they've perhaps needed me. It's only now, when I look at my fourth son, Stacey, I realise just what I've missed with my other kids. They've got a father whom they will never know as well as they should, and I've got flesh and blood whom I would dearly love to be closer to, but the situation is impossible. My only excuse is that I was young and naive. If I had my time again, that is the one thing that I would do differently because it kills me to think that I may ever have done something to hurt my children.

Thankfully, my teenage years at least saw me take my first steps to becoming a professional footballer, thanks to a side called Ten Em Bee. Around south London they were known as the business, as good as some of the semi-professional sides that were playing in the area and better than most of the other Saturday teams. I was playing for a youth club called Barracudas 80 but, although that was good for a year or so, people weren't taking it seriously and it began to fall apart when the guys who weren't so interested stopped showing up and we were left without a full side.

It was my friend, Aidan, who told me about Ten Em Bee and said I ought to go along and see if I was good enough. So there I was, Mr Cocky, thinking, 'Yeah, I'll have a game with them if they're up to scratch', and I went down to Penge to watch them play. I soon realised it wasn't a case of if they were good enough for me: rather, if I was good enough for them. They were the first organised black side that I had ever seen. There was only one white guy playing for them, a lad called called Johnny X who played down the left and had all the skill in the world. They played in the London and Kent Border League, and at the time they were one of the strongest sides around, with skill and strength and a brilliant team spirit.

I trained with them a few times and obviously impressed the manager, Tony Davies, because he signed me up, and that was the start of some of the best years I ever had playing football. I was the kid on the team, but all the other lads were around the same age, they all came from roughly the same area and we all shared the same sense of humour and attitude. It wasn't all refined silky skills, and you certainly learned to take care of yourself against some of the defenders in that league. They must have loved it when they saw me come out on a Saturday afternoon, cocky but still wet behind the ears, and more than a few of them laughed as they booted me up in the air for about the thousandth time. When you've played against some of those boys, nothing in the Premiership will ever worry you again!

But I put up with all the lumps, bumps and bruises and learned my trade. People say it's difficult to get into the pro game if you haven't done an apprenticeship at a club, but that was my apprenticeship, and I 'll tell you something, it doesn't come much harder anywhere else. You either grow up quick or get out, it's as simple as that, because there's no time for kids in the London and Kent Border League.

Luckily, as I said, I was surrounded by good players and once I got my best mate, Conrad Marquis, on the team, we were really on fire. Conrad and I had grown up together on the estate and had always played football together on the block. He was the supplier and I was the finisher, and we had a relationship where I knew when and exactly where he was going to cross or pass and I'd be on the end of it.

In the four years that I was with Ten Em Bee, we must have won at least one cup or league title every season. There were so many big games, but I remember the first final I was involved in with them was at Bromley Town against a side called Lomal who had Paul Elliott's two brothers, Jeff and Tony, playing for them. Conrad and I decided that we were going to do things properly and we both nicked a day off work, got dressed up in our best suits and went out and did the business on the pitch. I scored three that day and I think Conrad set two of them up, but I tell you we were unstoppable. We must have been pretty impressive because Jeff and Tony came to join us the next season and they were two excellent players.

The following year we won another cup and I got the winner in the final, and the year after that we won the Mary Wiltshire Shield which was the biggest cup competition around south London. I got a hat-trick in the semi-final against Paxton, and then another three in the final at Dulwich Hamlet's ground, and that had to be the highlight of my career at the time.

I was 19, and Tony Davies, a man who I love dearly and whom I would trust with my life, set me up for a trial with Brighton and my first real chance to show that I had what it took to be a professional. I wasn't working, and suddenly I had been presented with this chance, the opportunity that I thought had passed me by when I was at school. I'd never been so excited in all my life to think that a club might actually want me and that all I had to do was play well and train well and impress for two months. I knew I could do it: I knew I had what it took to become a professional.

For two months I set them alight at Brighton. Tony would drive me down and I would stay with him and his girlfriend. But after a while I started commuting, getting the bus to Victoria Station and then a train down to Brighton, work my balls off every day, and then come home again knowing I had done well. At the end of two months I knew in my heart that I had done more than enough to earn a contract. The Brighton players at the time, people like Perry Digweed and Chris Ramsay, were just telling me to accept whatever terms and wages the club offered, they were that sure I'd done enough.

But Chris Catlin, who was the manager at the time, saw it differently. He told Tony Davies to tell me that he didn't want me there. I was absolutely gutted. I would have cried if I hadn't been so angry. They chose an Irish kid called Steve Penney ahead of me, but – no disrespect to him – I was a street ahead during those two months. The only thing I can salvage from that time at Brighton is the fact that Chris Catlin is now probably selling sticks of rock on Brighton pier!

If the professional teams weren't showing any interest, then the semi-professional clubs in south London certainly were. Tony got me a trial at Fisher Athletic, the biggest club of their kind south of the Thames. At that time they were in the old Isthmian Premier League, on the verge of going up into the GM Conference which was just a step away from what used to be the Fourth Division. They were run by a guy called Dogan Arif.

Ten Em Bee played at the bottom of Fisher's ground in Bermondsey and Tony dragged me along to one of their games, went up to Arif and told him that he had a really good prospect who could do a job for Fisher. Without even turning around to look at me, Arif said, 'Yeah, just tell him to come along to one of our training sessions and I'll have a look at him.' That really pissed me off because I didn't think he had paid me any respect and didn't give a toss for either me or Tony. I still went along one Tuesday night, but I was late, and as I was getting off the bus I tripped on the kerb and twisted my ankle, so I couldn't even get my boots on, let alone train. A great first impression!

I thought that was it, no chance at Fisher, but my cousin Godfrey played for their reserves, and Arif, who had obviously heard of my reputation, kept asking him to get me down. Tony also thought I should go back for another session because he knew I could do well at that level. Just to get everybody off my back, I did return to Fisher, but I didn't take any kit. I just sat down at a table with Arif and the reserve team manager and said, 'I ain't gonna play for you because you didn't show me no respect the first time you met me. You didn't even turn round to look at me and you only want me now because you think I will score loads of goals for you. It was a blessing that I twisted my ankle and couldn't train. Now I'm off.' They just looked at me as if I was mad. They must have been thinking 'Who is this mouthy little bastard?'

By the time I was 21 I'd had quite a few jobs, mainly labouring ones on the building sites where I had learned to be a plasterer, but I was hardly lining my pockets with gold. But suddenly it seemed as if the whole world wanted to throw money at me! I had managed to land a job with Tunnel Refineries at Greenwich which, although it wasn't the most glamorous thing in the world, at least paid a pretty good whack. We worked in horrible conditions, up to our ankles in water most of the time, cleaning and repairing all sorts of tunnels and pipes, using chemicals which could strip the skin off your hands if you were stupid enough ever to remove your gloves and protective clothing. It was hard work but, as I say, it brought in £300 a week and I was pretty happy with that at the time.

Towards the end of the football season, Ten Em Bee were unable to get a pitch to play on for some reason, so we played a few matches down at Greenwich Borough. The manager there, Mick Wakefield, saw me play a few times and asked if I fancied playing for them in the remaining matches of their season. Tony Davies didn't mind so I think I played three matches for Greenwich and did pretty well, although the best part was picking up £30 per match. I couldn't believe it: someone actually wanted to pay me to play football!

At the end of the season, Mick took me to one side and said, 'Listen son, we aren't exactly rolling in dough, but if you join us next season I'll give you a hundred quid to sign on and twenty-five quid a game.' I was thinking, 'What's going on here? All this money just to play football!' but Tony had told me that Dulwich Hamlet were also interested and that I should speak to their manager, Bill Smith, and hear what he had to offer. So I played it cool and told Mick that I was going to speak to Dulwich. He knew I was just playing games, because I was in my element thinking so many clubs wanted me at long last. Bill Smith said that he would give me £150 to sign on and £20 a game, and suddenly these were mind-boggling figures, because nobody had given me 20 pence to play football before.

Yet while I was talking to Greenwich and Dulwich, Tony and his assistant, Errol Palmer, were working away at fixing up a trial with Crystal Palace, without me knowing anything about it. A Palace scout, Peter Prentice, had seen me play in a final at Dulwich's ground where I'd scored four goals and had really been on fire, and he'd told Tony that he'd like to take a look at me over a two-week trial period.

When I heard that, there was no question in my mind, I had to give it a shot. But Bill Smith, bless him, said 'If you go to Palace, they'll mess you about for six months, you won't go anywhere and then you'll be back to where you started from. Why don't you stay here, at least you'll be guaranteed a game and some reasonable money?' It was a good try and I told him if it didn't work out then I'd come back and sign for him, but I owed it to myself to try and finally crack it with the professionals. If it didn't work out, fine, I'd tell myself I'd had a go and that it wasn't to be, and get on with my life.

So in the summer of 1985, at the age of 21, I turned up at the Palace training ground in Colliers Wood to give it one last shot at the big time.

4
How to Get to Selhurst Park

I went for the trial at Palace with the attitude that this was going to be the last time I would put myself through all that agony, letting people pull me apart with their criticism and then getting rid of me as if I was just another piece of meat. I fully expected at the end of two weeks to be told the same old story, 'Nice try, son, but you're not what we're looking for.'

It was as if I was saying to myself, 'To hell with this, I don't need the hassle. If it doesn't work out, fine, but I'm bloody well going to show these bastards what a good player I am.' I went there relaxed, knowing I had a solid job to fall back on if things didn't work out, and if they did, all well and good. I had a good job with Tunnel Refineries in Greenwich and knew that I could earn a good wage even without football. It had been a toss-up whether or not I was actually going to go to the trial, but my boss, Gary Twydell, told me I had to go for it, and that I would never forgive myself if I wasted this opportunity. Bless him, he even promised to keep my job open if it didn't work out. That was the security I needed because my son, Bradley, had just been born and I knew that I needed a steady job to look after him and his mum.

There was no way that I could have played any better than I did during my trial at Brighton, and at the end of that I'd got a kick in the guts, nothing else. So if Palace were expecting the next Pele, they were going to be disappointed. But what they would get was a south London kid who was willing to work his socks off on his last chance.

Steve Coppell, then Palace manager, tells me now that he was completely shocked by my attitude. Normally triallists would come along a nervous wreck and leave exactly the same two weeks later. Steve reckons I was an arrogant little so-and-so who strutted around as if I owned the place, and that was what surprised all the other players. I got a little bit of respect for that, but Stevie, man, I'm telling you straight, I was as nervous as a kid starting his first day at school!

What I never told anybody at Palace was that Paul Elliott had set up a trial for me at Luton where he was playing. I'd known Paul for ages because he and his brothers were from the same part of London and all mixed in the same footballing circles, so he did me a favour and told Luton that I was worth a look at. I was supposed to be at Palace for a fortnight and then straight away go up to Luton for another couple of weeks. Whether that helped me to stay even more relaxed, I don't know, but it took away some of the focus from the Palace trial. I was relaxed: I just had it in my mind that I would play the way I played for Ten Em Bee and, if they didn't like it, tough. I wasn't going to pretend to be anybody other than Ian Wright, the striker. And that was exactly the thing that made the trial with Palace such a success: I wasn't trying to do what the professionals were doing, I was trying to show what I was good at.

In the training sessions I was working hard, I felt good and I knew that things were going well for me. A few of the players were really encouraging and told me to keep it up because they knew that Steve Coppell and the other staff were quietly impressed. At the end of the first week, a Palace XI had a game against Kingstonians and I was picked to play up front. I was on fire that day! I was doing everything, overhead kicks, taking everybody on and beating them for pace, and I even scored the winner. I came off knowing that I had played well and was doing all right for a trialllist.

Steve was at the game and while I was getting changed he came into the dressing room and took me to one side. 'Listen,' he said, 'I want you to report to Selhurst Park for the first-team friendly against Coventry.' I'll tell you, my jaw hit the ground! I could not believe it: ten days before I'd been thinking about whether to sign for Dulwich Hamlet or Greenwich Borough and now I was being asked to join the Palace first-team squad.

The only problem was ... I didn't know how to get to Selhurst Park. I know that sounds stupid, but even people who live in south London couldn't give directions to a stranger on how to get there; it has to be the best kept secret in the world. People know roughly where it is, but how to get there? That's another story. I didn't have a car so I had to rely on buses, and that was where my problems started. I caught a bus from my mum's in Forest Hill to Crystal Palace Parade, which I naturally thought couldn't be too far from the ground. I got off and asked some guy how to get to Crystal Palace, and the geezer sent me a mile in the wrong direction to Crystal Palace sports ground where they have all the big athletics meetings! That's all I needed – late for the biggest game of my life and just about to blow my best chance of making it. I got on another bus back up to the Parade and then another which took me to just down the road from Selhurst Park and from there I sprinted to the ground.

When I got there, Steve called me to one side and just said, 'Follow me.' We walked for a while without saying anything and then he just stopped, turned to me and said, 'We're going to sign you on for three months at £100 a week.' That was it; the world stopped turning for a few seconds while the news just sank in, and then I was just dancing around in delight: I had never been so happy in all my life. I had made it, the first step on the ladder, and it was all down to Steve. We've had our rows over the years, massive bust-ups at times, but I will never be able to thank that man enough for the chance that he gave me. I asked him a few years ago why he gave me only a three-month contract to start with, and he said that the club couldn't afford any more and that he had to fight just to give me a ton a week. Thank God he had that sort of faith in me. The thing that Steve liked about me was my freshness. I always wanted to try and do something different and he loved that. In my first trial match when we played against the first team, I just wanted to show people all the tricks that I had, and I really carved up some of the first-team defenders. I was nut-megging Jim Cannon, I turned Mickey Droy inside out and I showed up Dave Lindsay so badly that he poked me in the eye! The only one who could keep me in check and match me for pace was Henry Hughton, so I stayed away from his side of the pitch!

Ron Noades told me a story after I had left Palace about how Steve used to talk about me in my first few months as a Palace player. He would go up to Ron's office and say. 'There's a kid at training who's got all the tricks and can do great things, but he'll never be a player.' Then a couple of weeks later, he'd say, 'The kid is still doing well and he does some great things, he might make a player.' Then at the end of three months, he said to Ron, 'This boy is unbelievable, he will definitely make it as a player.'

Steve also knew I had an unshakeable belief in myself right from the first day. When he asked me what I wanted to do in football, I told him straight away that I was going to play for England. Not *wanted* to play for England, but definitely *going* to play for England. Steve likes that in a person and respects it.

Before the Coventry game, Steve took me up to his office and I signed the contract he put in front of me. I was shaking like a leaf and could hardly hold the pen, let alone write with it. Once all the signing was out of the way, I phoned my mum and told her the news and we both broke down, sobbing our hearts out: me because I was so happy to have made it, and her because she knew just how badly I wanted to be a footballer. Then I had to pull myself together and try to get a little bit of composure because I still had a game to play. I was one of the substitutes, and while I was sitting on the bench all I could do was think about getting out on the pitch as a real professional footballer, not just someone with dreams.

But I was suddenly having second thoughts within a minute or so of going on. Steve told me just to go out, relax and do what came naturally. The only thing that came naturally was me learning how to fly without the aid of wings or an engine, thanks to Brian Kilcline. 'Killer' was captain of Coventry and one of the most frightening defenders you'll ever come up against; he must have been about twenty feet tall with muscles on his breath, let alone his legs. He weighed the situation up within a second. Here was the fresh-faced striker who thought he had hit the big time, the perfect scenario for a big centre half to make his mark.

The first ball was played up to me out of defence and I knew exactly what I was going to do, flick it on with my head out to the wing, spin, and get in for the return ball, nice and easy. Killer had other ideas! Just as I was about to jump, BANG! I'm hit from behind by what I thought was a speeding juggernaut. I flew – and that's the only word for it – about twenty yards, landed in a heap and looked up to see Killer with a little smile on his face as if to say 'Welcome to the real world, son.'

I soon discovered that the real world in football meant picking up a lot more knocks, both physical and mental. I joined Palace when the dressing room was divided virtually down the middle between the seasoned old pros on one side and the young kids who were the future of the club on the other. It didn't help that a lot of the youngsters were black, people like Andy Gray, Tony Finnigan and myself. Now I will never be able to swear, hand on heart, that some of the older lads were prejudiced or just jealous of the fact that our careers were just starting and theirs were ending. What I do know is that the likes of Jim Cannon and George Wood seemed to single the young lads out and give them a really hard time.

Cannon opened my eyes to the fact that, even within a team, there is always going to be a divide, and the only time you're truly together is on a Saturday for ninety minutes. I remember playing a six-a-side training match where it was the old boys against the youngsters and we were absolutely slaughtering them. I beat somebody to go clear on goal and Cannon was there waiting on the line, as he always did – he never ventured very far forward, just stood on the line. I knew what I was going to do right from the start and, as he came towards me, I slipped the ball through his legs to score. That was it, I was celebrating, and turned away with my arm in the air. Suddenly, Cannon came up behind me and punched me in the back of the head and pushed my face down in the mud. He looked down at me and said, 'Don't ever do that again, you flash little c***'. I was so shocked, I almost wanted to cry. I couldn't believe that somebody who was supposed to be part of a team would act like that just because his ego was dented. It was a tough lesson to learn and one that would always stick with me.

Looking back, it was probably a case of the old pro's trying to teach the kids a thing or two about life, but at the time I couldn't handle it. Things got so bad with players having a go at each other – and I mean seriously kicking each other – that Steve Coppell had to call a meeting to sort it out. That didn't really help because he couldn't hide the fact that he liked Andy, Tony and the rest of the youngsters, so in training it was a case of the senior players saying, 'Oh, we mustn't touch Stevie's little boys or they'll go crying to the gaffer.'

George Wood really couldn't stand us, and Andy in particular. Now anybody who knows Andy will tell you that he is not slow in coming forward and will give you his opinion whether you want it or not. In training he was never frightened to have his say or have a go at somebody, even the boss. I don't think the older players understood his character or liked the way he talked to the staff, because in their day it was a case of 'don't speak unless you're spoken to'. Suddenly there was this kid telling Steve what he thought and that wound the older boys up.

Things reached a head on a pre-season tour of Sweden just a year after I signed as a professional. There had been the usual round of wind-ups, and rows, but George decided he'd had enough. Andy and Tony were sharing a room and were in it watching TV late one night while George was downstairs in the bar getting absolutely slaughtered. He didn't take a lot of firing up at the best of times, but after he'd had a few drinks and the rest of the players were winding him up, telling him the jumped-up Flash Harrys needed sorting out, he took it upon himself to do the sorting. He stormed up to Andy's room and just started kicking at the door and screaming how he was going to teach Andy a lesson. Andy was frightened, even he will admit that, but he let George in and just started talking and talking, trying to calm him down and talk George out of giving him and Tony a hammering. Eventually George did calm down and left them alone, but for a few minutes it was rather unpleasant. Both Andy and Tony came into my room after George had gone back to the bar, and they were shaken up, man, because they knew how close they'd come to an ugly scene.

It wasn't the nicest atmosphere in the world to start your professional career, but the good times outweighed the bad on the whole. After three months, Steve called me into his office again and told me that the club were willing to extend my contract to a year and pay me £250 a week. This time I wasn't as surprised as when I had first signed, but I was just as pleased, although the boss, in his own way, kept my feet on the ground when he said, 'Now you can afford to take your girlfriend out for a meal ... to McDonald's!' I know that was his way of telling me not to get carried away too much or to get too flash.

But the 1985/86 season is the one that I will remember for the rest of my life. God has blessed me by making me a footballer and helping me to win lots of medals and England caps, but I will never thank Him as much as I did when I scored my first professional goal for Palace. I'd been on the bench for the first two or three games of the season and didn't get on until we played Huddersfield away. Then I came on against Fulham at Selhurst Park and did quite well in a 0–0 draw and I think the fans began to take an interest in me because I was young and enthusiastic and would chase everything when I came on as a substitute.

The next game was against Oldham at home and I was on the bench again. There were about seventy minutes gone and we were losing 2–1 when suddenly I heard the crowd chanting 'Ian Wright! Ian Wright! Ian Wright!' ... and in the next moment the boss was telling me to get stripped and warmed up as I was going on. He just told me to work hard and try and make a difference, and that's exactly what I did. The Oldham defenders didn't really know how to handle me because I was fresh and quick, and I managed to cause them all sorts of problems. After about five minutes, I turned and played a ball through to Kevin Taylor who hit it and it screamed in, a blinding goal to level things up.

Then, with about three minutes to go, Alan Irvine got the ball out on the left and I peeled away to the back post. Alan hung the ball up perfectly for me and I got above the Oldham defender who was trying to mark me and headed it down past the keeper. The feeling I had at that moment will never ever leave me. Whatever goals I score, whether it's to win cup finals or for my country, they will never be quite as special as that one, it was simply amazing, fairy-tale stuff that I couldn't describe. Not only had I made a difference to the match, I'd actually scored the winner, and I'll tell you something, nobody could catch me. I ran from the six-yard box right to the halfway line, just screaming with delight. I had scored, and I felt as though I'd arrived, I was part of something.

My mum and brothers were all in tears when they were listening to the score flashes on the radio, and the next day the papers were full of how I was a 'Supersub' who had come on and saved Palace. The Supersub tag stuck with me because for the next few games Steve held me back and kept me on the bench, just throwing me on when he thought we needed something different. Invariably I would score, and we got a little run going thanks to my goals.

I suppose I should have known that not everybody was going to be pleased with the way things were going for me, and Jim Cannon made sure that nothing had changed off the pitch. He may have been picking up win bonuses thanks to my goals, but that didn't stop him giving me a hard time all the same. He'd always be there with the snide comments, telling me I was only a twenty-minute player, that I couldn't do it for the whole match. I should have been flying high, but his teasing and digs were sapping my confidence. I even began to wonder whether he was right and that I couldn't do it for the whole ninety minutes. It wasn't that I doubted my own ability because I knew that I could score goals, but I needed to prove to Cannon and anybody else that I wasn't just a flash in the pan, that I was a footballer, not a three-minute wonder.

I scored nine goals in 32 games in my first season which wasn't bad going, considering that I didn't start too many matches, and the boss told me that he was pleased with the way I was learning and coming on. Halfway through the season, he'd extended my contract from a year to three years and had shown a lot of faith in me, a raw kid from the streets who had only been in the game nine months. But he could see that I wasn't going to be able to do it for Palace all on my own, that I needed a partner who I could play with and spark off. So he made one of the best decisions a Crystal Palace manager will ever make: he went out and bought Mark Bright, and, from then on, neither the club nor myself looked back.

'Brighty'and I were a match made in heaven right from the start. He was from a completely different background to me, but we just hit it off straight away because our characters just moulded together. He started off at Leek Town, then went on to his local side, Port Vale, before joining Leicester City where he was playing in the same side as Gary Lineker. Brighty picked so much up off Lineker, it's unbelievable. When he came to Palace, he knew how to behave, how to react to situations and how to carry himself at all times. He is one of the deepest thinkers I've ever met in football. He's got the sort of brain that can see situations before they're even happening and he knows exactly where to go and what to do to make the most of them. Where I'm instinctive and do things even though I don't know why sometimes, he always does things for a reason, and he drilled that into me right from the start of our partnership.

When Steve signed him, Brighty wasn't having the best of times at Leicester. The crowd were getting on his back and he wasn't getting a regular place in the side, so he was looking to get away. He laughs about it now, but Brighty used to get abused in the street and on the pitch; fathers would even bring their kids along to reserve team games just to let them watch Brighty so they could practise giving stick to players.

Steve told him that Palace were a young team going places and that he felt that if Brighty and myself could hit it off, then we would be unstoppable, because our natural style of play would gel together. He needed a new challenge, I needed

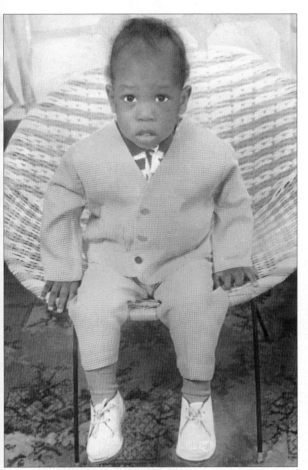

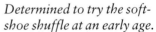
Always a style leader! Three years old and I'm already suited and booted.

Determined to try the soft-shoe shuffle at an early age.

A happy family at home with brother Morris and my mum Nesta.

Teenage rampage. Aged fourteen and ready for action on the south London streets.

Above: Take aim and fire! There's no better feeling than knowing it's a goal as soon as you've hit the ball. Playing for Palace, I had a lot of practice!

Right: Pure sax! It's the best way I've found of relaxing … although the jazz greats haven't got much to worry about.

Below: The dream team. Brighty and I were a brilliant striking partnership for the Eagles – we had a telepathic understanding at times.

Above: Let's go mental. We've just beaten Spurs in an FA Cup semi-final at Wembley in 1993, so it doesn't get much better than this.

Below: Arsenal v Sheffield Wednesday at Wembley in May 1993. This is the stuff that dreams are made of, scoring in an FA Cup Final. Shame it wasn't the winner.

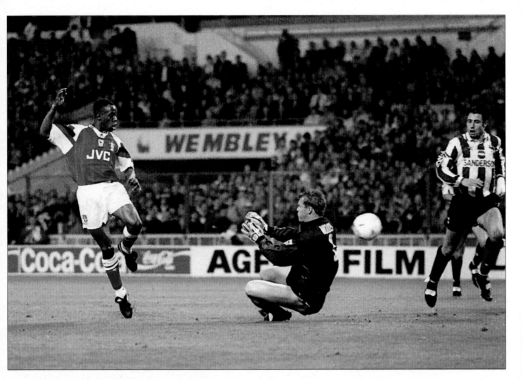

Above: Sheffield Wednesday cop for it again, this time in the Cup Final replay a fortnight later, as I make it four goals in four finals and Arsenal clinch the trophy after a 2–1 win.

Below: So many thoughts go through your mind when you're stretchered off like this. The agony of breaking my leg in 1990 is something I'll never forget.

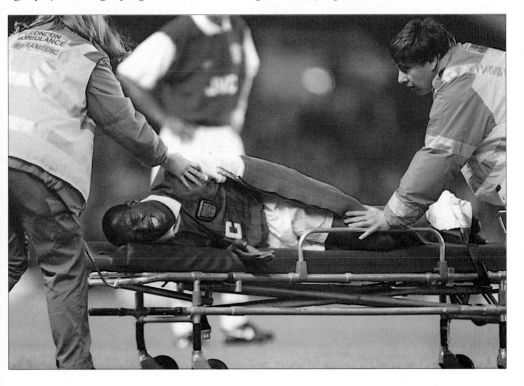

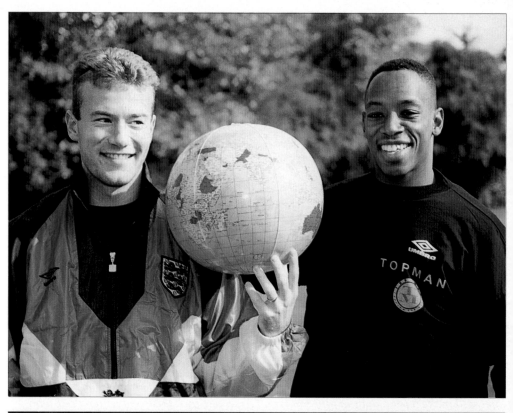

Above: The lowest of the lows as we troop off after a 1–0 defeat against the United States – of all the teams to lose against!

Right: Picking up splinters in my backside … the story of my England career.

Opposite, above: Alan Shearer and I could have made a great partnership for England, except that Graham Taylor had different ideas.

Opposite: One of the most important goals of my life as I get England out of jail in Poland during a World Cup qualifying match in September 1993.

Above: For once I've outdone him as far as suits go! Me and Chris Eubank.

Right: Gangsta Style. Hip man as a hit man.

Below: Front foot forward, head over the ball, perfect grip. I lack just one thing where cricket's concerned – talent.

somebody older and more experienced to show me what being a striker was really about, and thank God he decided to sign. Right from day one, he was on my case, giving me instructions, telling me what runs to make and why. I remember during one of our first sessions together he suddenly turned round and said, 'Look at yourself, look how muddy you are. That's because you're always falling over when you pass or shoot. Now look at me, look how clean I am; that's because I stay on my feet so I can be in position to get a pass or have another shot.' And that stuck with me and I tried hard to be like him, balanced and in control all the time, not like some wild and grubby urchin running around like a headless chicken.

The first game we played together was brilliant, and justified Steve's decision to play us together. We were playing Ipswich, and Mark had scored on his debut, but we were losing 3–1 and my head had gone. Nothing had been going right for me, all my passes went astray and it was as if Ipswich had an extra player – except he was wearing a Crystal Palace shirt. But Brighty just kept on at me all through the game. He kept telling me to make the same runs, keep doing the right thing and something would come from it. Suddenly Kevin Taylor pulled one back for us and my game started to come together and I realised that Brighty was right. Just to make sure I learned a true lesson, I scored the equaliser with a few minutes to go and he just looked over as if to say, 'Told you so.' From that moment on, I had the utmost respect for him and everything he said. I can't count the number of times during games when I've lost my head and become so frustrated when things weren't going right, and Brighty has called me over, told me concentrate on the game and what I'm supposed to be doing, and it has all come right in the end. He is brilliant at that, at knowing that you must never stop making runs or passes because in the one split-second that everything clicks, you could score the winning goal at

Wembley and be a hero instead of just a footballer. Even now when I've done something stupid, he'll phone me up and say, 'What the hell did you do that for? Why doesn't anything get through your thick head?' And I have to hold my hands up and admit that he's right.

From the start we were mates off the pitch as well, because our characters complemented each other. I didn't realise how close we were until a nasty incident in training shortly after Brighty had arrived. It was another old boys against youngsters match, and we were giving them the run-around and not worrying how badly we showed them up. Gavin Nebbeling was getting the worst of it because he was chasing the ball from one of us to another and not getting anywhere near it. Brighty couldn't help himself and pointed at Gavin and called out, 'Mad Dog.' Gavin just squared up to him and said, 'What did you say?' and before Brighty could open his mouth, Gavin butted him square in the face. Everybody was shocked, Gavin more than anybody and he walked straight off back to the changing rooms. The thing was, I felt so helpless because I couldn't do anything to help Mark or even say anything that would make it right. Jim Cannon and all the older players were all muttering to themselves how it served Brighty right, and there was Mark with blood pouring down his face and I couldn't do anything. From that moment on, I felt closer to Brighty than I've ever done with any other player.

5
Wright and Bright

Mark Bright joined Palace in November of the 1986/87 season when the club were seriously struggling. We needed something to spark us, and his arrival seemed to do that; it certainly gave me the sort of lift that spurred me on, because things weren't exactly on fire as far as my scoring form was concerned. Everybody seems to think that the Bright and Wright headlines started straight away, but that just wasn't the case because Palace weren't doing anything to get the headlines except struggling to stay alive in the old Second Division.

When Mark did sign, Steve took us to one side and told us that we were the two players who could make a difference to the club and he didn't care how much stick he got from the rest of the players, he was going to centre Palace's game on the pair of us. That was a brave decision and a gamble on his behalf, but we had enough faith in our own ability and the understanding that we had struck up to say, 'Yeah Boss, that's the right thing.'

It caused some friction in the dressing room, there's no doubt about that. Because Brighty and I played closely together and socialised all the time off the pitch, the other lads were always digging at us about being only interested in ourselves and not in the team. There was an element of that, but it's only natural in strikers. If there's one glory position on the pitch, it's centre forward, and you have to have that bit of ego and self-confidence in yourself to be a successful striker.

I have never seen one top striker who has not had the selfish streak in him. Anybody who plays up front and says that they're happy to see the team win even if they don't score is a liar. Sometimes you say that to the media because you don't want the big-headed image to come over in the papers or on the television, but deep in your heart you know it's rubbish. I am desperate for goals: they're what my job is all about, and if I'm not scoring – even if the team is winning – I sulk, and Brighty is exactly the same. The thrill of seeing the ball hit the back of the net and a goalkeeper lying helpless on the ground is a sight that always gets my blood pumping to such an extent that often I can't control myself and I do silly, crazy celebrations. I may look like an idiot when I'm celebrating but I don't care because I've put the ball in the back of the net and I'm in heaven!

Sadly, as I said, there wasn't too much delight at first for either Brighty or myself. While we clicked off the pitch straight away, every on-pitch partnership needs work, and we had to put the hours in on the training pitch. I've always loved training. When I first signed as a professional I felt guilty about knocking off at 12.30 or one o'clock every day, especially as I was used to working until six virtually every night. I got rid of that guilt by staying behind to work in the afternoons with anybody who was around.

Sometimes Steve would come out and we'd work on finishing or positional play and anything I could think of to improve my game. If he wasn't about or too busy to work on the pitch, I'd grab some unsuspecting apprentice or reserve team player and get him to feed crosses in at all heights and angles just so I could improve my finishing. I must have driven a few of the kids mental because I would never stop until I had got it absolutely right with my head and both feet.

It's something I still do now at Arsenal, along with Paul Merson and Dennis Bergkamp, because no matter how far up the tree you get, you can always go further. Bruce Rioch's catchphrase is 'You never got worse by practising' and although I must have heard it a thousand times, it still makes perfect sense.

When Brighty arrived at Palace, we were always out late at night and most times we'd drag John Salako out with us. He was a few years younger than us but even then we could see he was going to be a great player. He was intelligent and could cross a ball superbly, mostly from the left, but he was pretty good off his right side as well. John got a hard time from us because we're both perfectionists, and if he wasted a cross we went to town on him. I think he was pleased to be asked along but scared that he'd make a mistake, which to my mind is a good thing. John might not agree, but a bit of fear at the back of your mind helps you concentrate so much more! Although Brighty and I used to slaughter John if he ever did something wrong, we also used to look after him. Thanks to us, he must have been the best-dressed young footballer in London when we began to take off as a partnership. Brighty and I have always been well into fashion and once we could afford it, we'd hit the shops in a big way every month or so, splashing out on the latest designer gear. When John broke into the first team we would take him aside before games and tell him that if he set a goal up for either of us, we'd give him a pair of shoes, a jacket or some trousers that we didn't wear any more. You should have seen him: he was only earning about £250 a week but he was decked out in Armani, Hugo Boss, the lot. It would have cost him a month's wages just for one arm of a jacket, but he got it all for nothing providing he did the business for us on a Saturday afternoon.

Don't get the idea that Brighty and I always saw eye to eye just because we were close off the pitch. On the pitch it was a different story. He used to tell me that whatever position he took up, I should always know exactly where to run, to the extent of being almost telepathic. And most of the time it worked a treat. If he pulled out wide and got the ball then I always ran to the near post for a whipped in cross behind the defence but in front of the goalie. If I got the ball on the left and cut inside on my right foot, then I wouldn't have to look up – I just clipped a ball to the back post where he would have pulled off the centre half. When he went up for the first challenge from a ball out of defence, then I knew where my run should be to collect the flick-on if he won it. Sounds simple, but sometimes instinct would take over and I'd gamble on something different happening, and if it didn't come off Brighty would go mental. I've heard him shout so many times during a match, 'Ian, what the f*** do you think you're doing? We all know you can beat three players once in a match, but why don't you just do the simple things properly?' That's when I'd go mad myself and turn round to him and ask him who the hell he thought he was talking to. That just brought out the school teacher in him and he'd look at me as if I was a naughty pupil and say, 'Wrighty, there's ten other players on the park as well as you.' I couldn't handle that and I'd want to give him some back, but every time I'd start to say something Brighty would ask, 'Am I right or am I wrong?' and there was no argument ... he was always right!

But if we gave each other a hard time, then it was nothing to the abuse defenders got from us. Neither one of us are nasty players and I don't think we have done too many things that we'd be ashamed of when we're retired. I know Brighty got involved with Andy Linighan in the FA Cup Final replay when Arsenal played Sheffield Wednesday, but Andy got his own back when he scored the winner in the last minute. A busted-up nose is a small price to pay for scoring the winner at Wembley. Although there's nothing malicious about us, we would always let defenders know we were about, physically and verbally. The first challenge was always important because the centre halves marking us always found out we were around. And we never let up in the verbals either, and Brighty was the master of it. I can be just plain abusive, but he's the master of the cruel one-liner, and you can see the defender's face drop a mile after he's made a mistake when Brighty shouts over to me, 'Ian, go easy on him today, the bloke's doing badly enough without you upsetting him'; or sometimes he would just give it a plain and simple, 'Never mind, big man, there's always next week,' as he shook his head almost in sympathy.

We were also a perfect double act with the verbal abuse. If we were up against a defender who likes to chat all the way through a game, nothing made us laugh more than just winding him up. I don't know why, but they always seemed to speak to Brighty first. It was always, 'All right Brighty, how's it going?' And he would go, 'F*** off, if you want to talk, see me in the bar afterwards.' That would shock the defender and he'd slide over to mark me. Now I didn't want to give the game away so I made sure he never saw me laughing, and when he asked 'What's up with your mate today?' I'd give him another volley like 'Get lost, I didn't come here to talk to you, you muppet.' You could see the pain and confusion in their faces, and that gave us an edge that we could exploit later on in the game. Sometimes it didn't work and you paid for it with a few extra bruises, but those occasions were few and far between.

We never planned to be Bright and Wright off the pitch as well as on it: that just seemed to happen naturally. We teamed up with Andy Gray and Tony Finnigan and had some wicked fun in those early days. We went everywhere together – Crazy Larry's in the Cromwell Road on a Tuesday, the Café de Paris on a Wednesday and Brown's on a Saturday night after a game; it was an exciting time and we were always there together. Brighty and I bought clothes together, we bought cars together and we'd go out together. He had a flat in Battersea (although he always called it south Chelsea!) and I still lived near my mum in Forest Hill, so on a Sunday we would both go to her house and have dinner, then if my friends and family were having a get-together at a local park or down the pub, we would be there. When I look back, those were some great days.

People say we were the new breed of footballers, and that was true to an extent. We were young and, unlike the generation before us, we had quite a lot of money. For Brighty and me that meant being able to spend it on clothes, and could we spend! Fashion has always been a very important part of my life and I think it has been for Mark as well. When I was at school, your social standing depended 99 per cent on what you wore and how you wore it. It didn't matter that your mum and dad didn't have two bob to rub together, if you looked smart, if you looked the business, then you were respected, even if your trainers didn't cost £50.

I remember doing a fashion photo spread in a newspaper with Mark just after we began to make the headlines as a duo. It was the first time I had appeared anywhere but the sports pages, and I was so proud that I was being recognised not just as a footballer but as a person with other interests. My mum gave me a hard time but I know she was just as proud, and I've got a sneaking suspicion she's got a cutting of that paper knocking around her house somewhere.

Despite the fact that Mark and I were building up a relationship and a partnership, we didn't exactly set the world alight that first season together. I only got eight goals in 38 games and Brighty hit the same but in 10 games fewer, so we weren't frightening the life out of defences. Palace finished halfway up the old Second Division which wasn't too bad because for the early part of the season we'd been in the relegation zone and most people were saying we had no chance of survival. There were times that season when I wondered if I really was good enough to be a professional, let alone play at the top, but Steve got hold of me around Christmas time and told me to keep concentrating on what I did best and everything would come good.

Even then he had a long-term plan for Palace that most of the players and virtually all the supporters failed to realise, but it was one that he would put into operation during the summer of 1987. He had already started the ball rolling: Brighty and I were working together as a partnership up front; the midfield looked pretty solid with Andy Gray, Alan Pardew and Phil Barber maintaining their consistency; and Gary O'Reilly was a rock at the back. But the boss knew that we had to strengthen the squad if we were going to get out of Division Two. That summer he really did the business in the transfer market. He bought Geoff Thomas and John Pemberton from Crewe, and keeper Perry Suckling from Manchester City, all within the space of a couple of months. Suddenly there were three new pieces to the jigsaw, and when we came back for pre-season training you could see that the new boys were going to fit in well.

Geoff and 'Pembo' were both northerners so they were mocked for their dopey accents, especially by Andy and I who were brought up together in the same part of south London with Tony Finnigan. Brighty may have been from Stoke, but he was now an honorary Londoner so he got off lightly, but Geoff and Pembo got some serious abuse. Geoff handled it well – he had a quick, dry sense of humour and could give as good as he got – but Pembo was a different matter. He was so easy to wind up and had a temper that snapped after just a couple of minutes. I love him dearly and will always remember his impression of the Road Runner in the FA Cup semi-final against Liverpool which set up one of our goals, but he and I had some major rows on the pitch and at the training ground, and I can't count the number of times we had to be stopped from belting the life out of each other. If he messed up a cross or ran into some blind alley, I'd lay into him and he'd give me some back. Then it would be all off and we'd be squaring up to each other, eyeball to eyeball, until one of the other players took it into their heads to keep us apart. There was never any actual physical violence but we got very close to it!

You'd never think, with all the abuse, the threats and the aggression that went on amongst us, that there was much of a team spirit at Palace, but, looking back, they were some of the happiest times that I've ever had in football. Everybody got on, we'd all go out together, our wives and families would socialise and it was just a great laugh. There weren't the hang-ups that other teams have or the cliques in the dressing room. It was just as if a bunch of mates had got together to play: magic days.

Brighty and I used to get called 'the golden boys' or 'Coppell's favourites' in the banter, but we just turned round and said, 'Where did your last win bonus come from?' and that was that, end of argument! The only real friction was between Geoff and Andy and that was because both of them wanted to be recognised as the top midfielder in the club, the man who bossed things on the park. To be fair, Geoff was pretty easy-going, but anybody who knows Andy will tell you that he can be the most awkward bastard in the world.

I'd never have a bad word said against him because I love him like a brother, but there were times when he'd even embarrass me. I used to hate going down to dinner with him on away trips because he'd give the poor waiter or waitress so many problems, it would be horrible to sit with him. He'd always ask for a steak with a fried egg on it and chips. You knew exactly what would happen, he'd cut into the egg and it would be too runny, so the waiter would have to take the egg off and have another one cooked. Then the steak would be too rare and he'd call the waiter over again and say, 'How am I supposed to eat this steak? It's still running around.' So back went the steak but Andy would insist on them leaving the chips which he would eat. Then the steak and egg would come back without any chips and he'd look up and say, 'How am I supposed to eat that without any chips? If my missus served it up like that she'd be wearing it or combing it out of her hair. Take it back.'

And he always had to be different from everybody else. I remember one episode with a sheepskin coat that still kills me to think about. It was a bitterly cold day and everybody had tracksuits, thermals, the lot, to train in. Not Andy. He found a manky sheepskin coat that had been left in the dressing rooms months before and which nobody ever owned up to leaving. It was the most disgusting thing you've ever seen, but Andy insisted on wearing it to try and keep warm. The problem was that Andy is a big guy and this coat was made for somebody half his size, but still he came out, collar turned up and buttons straining, just so he could say that he was warmer than anybody else. The geezer was mad!

I can't believe how well Steve Coppell handled all those guys – it was as if he was the man pulling the strings without us really knowing he was in control. There were some strong personalities in the dressing room and he just let us get on with it most of the time until things went too far. Then he'd be in, stamping his authority on things and telling us we were out of order and letting us know just exactly how far we could push things without the situation boiling over. I've tried to take a lot from him personality-wise, and also from the chairman, Ron Noades. I like the direct, positive way Steve deals with things, and he'll tell you exactly what's going to happen and why. Ron is also very direct, but he's also got a very aggressive kind of attitude, and if you don't like it, then tough, because that's the way it's going to be. They've both been very influential on my life, not just my footballing career, and taking those things from their personalities has sometimes got me in trouble because I tell reporters the way it is, and often that gets twisted to make massive headlines. But I can handle that because I know in my heart I've been honest and true to myself.

The 1987/88 season was a bedding-in year for Palace. We had the talent but we didn't quite have the consistency to make a real run for promotion. For a long time we were right up there, and Brighty and I hit the kind of scoring form that strikers as a pair only dream about. There was hardly a defence in the country that could stop us as a partnership; if they blanked me out, then Brighty would always pop up, and if Brighty was neutralised, I would come up with the goods. Suddenly we were both fulfilling our potential, and the supporters and the headline-writers were loving it. I scored 20 league goals at the rate of one every two games, plus another half-dozen in cup competitions, and Brighty did even better. He scored 25 goals in 38 games and must have set up easily half of mine with knock-downs or passes in the penalty area. It was as if we were twins separated at birth and were celebrating meeting up after all those years: everything we tried came off and we were untouchable.

When I think of the stick I get now from Palace fans when I go back to Selhurst Park with all their 'Judas' chants and abuse, it makes me wonder about their mentality. They accuse me of selling out to go to Arsenal, but what they forget is that both Brighty and I could have gone at the end of the 1987-88 season because there were enough clubs queuing up to take us, and I mean big clubs. I know Arsenal and Spurs were interested in me, Chelsea wanted Brighty and Liverpool looked at us both, but we didn't swagger around and storm in to demand a transfer when we really could have. Instead we both signed new contracts and told Steve Coppell that we wanted to stay at Palace because we loved what was happening with the club. In my heart I know I showed loyalty to the club and so did Mark. Fans want it all their way every time. Of course they want the best players to stay at the club, but then after five or six good years of service, they cannot respect that a player wants to better himself in his playing standards and financially. It's crazy: none of the values of real life matter where fans are concerned. Tell me, if somebody was offered a better job, with a company car and a massive wage rise plus an extra week's holiday and BUPA, would they turn it down? No, they'd be mugs to, so why should a footballer be any different? I love the passion and enthusiasm and love that fans bring to the game, but sometimes it's a hell of a job trying to make them see sense.

The 1987/88 season made us all realise that, with a bit more consistency, we could get promoted, no problem. There was nobody in that division that frightened us, no defence that could stop Brighty and me, and when the boss went out and signed Jeff Hopkins from Fulham in the summer, we suddenly had a defence of our own that was absolutely rock solid. I've never met another player who could match Jeff for honesty, courage and commitment. If I ever become a manager, he is the sort of player that I would want in my side before all your Fancy Dan footballers who haven't got anything near the guts that Jeff had. He is one of the most dedicated and underrated players I've ever met, and without him Palace might not have achieved as much as they did.

Suddenly everything clicked for us. Brighty and I started the next season as if there had never been a break, and right from the start of the season we knew that we were good enough to go up. But believing we were good enough to go up and proving it were two different things entirely because by Christmas we were in more danger of going down than pushing for promotion: things were that bad. We were all tearing our hair out wondering what the hell we had to do to turn things around when BOSH! the lights came on and we started buzzing. Brighty seemed to be scoring at will, I was scoring goals every time the ball came to me, and midfield and defence were absolutely outstanding. We must have gone on a run of thirteen or fourteen games unbeaten that lifted us from about sixth from bottom to third from top. It was incredible. There must have been a spell on us that made us unbeatable from the New Year onwards, right through Easter and towards the end of the season.

It came down to the last few games and things were so tight that you had to get a calculator out just to figure out how many goals you had to score or the others had to concede to make a difference. The last day of the season we played Birmingham at Selhurst and it was carnival time, or so it seemed. The Birmingham fans all came down in fancy costume, our fans were fired up because we had a chance to go up automatically if things went right, and we, as players, knew that this was a chance for our shot at the big time. Forgive me if I can't remember the exact mathematics of it all, but if we beat Birmingham by something like four clear goals and Manchester City lost or drew, then we could go up as champions. If they won, and we won, then Palace were in the play-offs. Nothing was simple, I can tell you that!

We started the game as if this was our World Cup final and we were the best team on earth: I have never know anything like it. We were 4–0 up in the first 35 minutes and I'd scored a hat-trick within half an hour. I'd had three shots and they'd all gone in – bang, bang, bang. The amazing thing was, we weren't celebrating the goals, we were just running to get the ball out of the net so we could start again and score some more. In the end we won comfortably, but it didn't matter because Manchester City won as well, so they went up automatically and we were in the play-offs. But the memory that will stay with me from that game came after the final whistle went and the Birmingham fans – in fancy dress, remember – decided to invade the pitch and confront the Palace boys. It will stay with me for ever: Adolf Hitler chasing a nun, with a policeman on horseback chasing the pair of them!

The play-offs were something else. We had to play Swindon over two legs, with the first match being at their place and we lost 1–0. I travelled back to London with David Rocastle who is a few years younger than me but went to the same school and is from the same area. He told me not to worry because we were good enough to beat them at home without too much problem.

The return leg was the following Wednesday and it was a really hot, hazy evening. I'd never played in front of so many people before and it seemed that everybody in the crowd was as hyped up as the players, as if they knew that something special was going to happen. When the Palace team come out on the pitch, the club play the song 'Glad All Over' and the crowd stamp their feet to the two beats just before the chorus. That night I thought the whole stadium was going to cave in, the noise was so loud.

The match went like a dream. Brighty scored to put us ahead after the goalkeeper fumbled. Normally he doesn't go wild when he scores, he's his normal calm self, but this time the veins in his neck were standing out and he was like a crazy man as we all jumped on him. Then we got a free kick about forty yards out: it was clipped in to Mark who flicked it on and I got in beyond the defenders to volley it home. I have never known such exhilaration and joy, because there was no way Swindon were going to get back from that. The crowd poured onto the pitch at the end and it was a mad dash to get down to the tunnel before we were mobbed to death.

That set up a home-and-away with Blackburn. These were the days before Kenny Dalglish and Jack Walker were spending big money, but they were still the favourites. We went up there and played like amateurs for most of the match, and they were 2–0 up before we'd even got ourselves going. At half-time, we were all going mad, pointing fingers and calling each other names, ready to put the blame on anybody else, when Steve calmed us all down and told us not to worry, and that one goal would be good enough as long as we didn't let in another.

We went out pumped up and ready for it, and that was when Jeff Hopkins really carved out a place for himself. Time was slipping away when a ball was crossed into the box and Jeff went for it, knowing full well that their keeper, Terry Gennoe, was odds-on to splatter him all over Ewood Park. But Jeff still went for it, the ball spun loose and Eddie 'Charlie Chaplin' McGoldrick was there to shoot home. I thought 'Sweet man, that's the goal we needed, now we'll get them at home.' What I didn't bank on was Howard Gayle popping up in the last few minutes to make it 3–1. If the atmosphere in the dressing room at half-time was bad, this time it was simply dreadful. We all wanted to kill each other. We called each other every name under the sun, and how Steve stopped a massive brawl breaking out, I'll never know. I was totally depressed because I could see my chance of the big time slipping away, and there was nothing I could do about it.

The match at Selhurst was one that I will never forget as long as I live. The atmosphere was even more incredible than for the Swindon game and there looked like 100,000 people packed in to the ground. For all the world it looked like a Cup Final crowd. I knew then that we couldn't let ourselves or these fans down, we'd come too far not to give them what they wanted. None of the players needed motivating: the boss might as well have gone home and watched the game on the telly because he didn't need to say anything.

My mum says that she loves the referee George Courtney because he always seems to favour whatever side I'm playing in, and on that day it looked as if he was a Palace fan. I'd pulled one back to make it 3–2 after a great cross from Alan Pardew, and Brighty had missed it. Then in the second half Eddie went on one of his mazy little runs, lost the ball and just seemed to fall over. There was hardly a Blackburn player near him, but George pointed straight to the spot, no hesitation. Dave Madden stepped up to take the penalty and suddenly his last two flashed through my mind, They were really poor efforts that somehow each goalkeeper managed to dive over or was so surprised that anybody could hit such a muffed shot that it trickled in. So I was just praying that he'd make a better fist of it this time, and the boy didn't let me down! It was a sweet connection that went straight in the bottom corner, and we were alive again.

In all the chaos, I'd lost count of the score and was just wandering around asking people what we needed to do. What we needed was a goal and, with a few minutes to go, Eddie headed for the touchline down the right and clipped over a perfect hanging cross straight onto my head with no defenders near me. All I had to do was steer it past Gennoe and into the bottom corner for one of my easiest goals of the season.

It may have been easy but it caused madness when the final whistle went. I'd always looked at teams being mobbed on the pitch when they've gone up, and wanted to find out what it was like. I found out all right, and it was one of the most moving experiences of my life. The fans carried me shoulder high to the tunnel and ripped every last item of clothing off me except my jock strap! All I could do when I got into the dressing room was cry and hug everybody who came near me because my wish had come true: I was going to play in Division One where it really mattered.

6
That Night
at Anfield

My first season in the top flight amongst the big boys brought the biggest humiliation I have ever known as a footballer, but also one of the greatest thrills of my life. To go to Anfield and lose 9–0 – and be lucky to get nil – was the lowest point of my whole career. Thank God it was cancelled out by scoring in an FA Cup Final, something I had dreamed about since I was five years old. That season also saw me get England recognition for the first time in front of my own people in my manor, Millwall.

But I'll tell you, man, before a ball was kicked, I was petrified. I was scared that I was going to let myself down, that I couldn't live with the best in England; it seemed that all that had gone before it was just preparation, this was the real thing. Anybody who knows me will say that I've got a tremendous self-confidence, but in the build-up to that season I was as nervous as I've ever been.

Think about it. There I was, the street kid who four years earlier was wondering whether to play for Dulwich Hamlet in front of a couple of hundred people, now going out to play against Manchester United at Old Trafford with 40,000 screaming northerners ready to give me some vicious abuse. It should have inspired me: instead I felt overawed and completely unsure of myself.

The first game didn't help, Palace losing 1–0 to a Paul Wright goal at QPR with the prospect of Manchester United coming to Selhurst Park in four days' time. But that was the game when I finally realised that if I didn't go out and show people what I was made of then I would get trampled all over, because Bryan Robson doesn't care that you're fresh out of the Second Division. All he wants to do is win and he'll do what it takes to get those points and have no sympathy.

You can't afford to go around with stars in your eyes. When I first went to play against Arsenal at Highbury, I just could not believe that place, and I could not believe that I would ever play for a club like Arsenal. But as soon as you step out onto the pitch you have to put those thoughts behind you because Tony Adams is waiting round the corner and if anybody can concentrate your mind, it's Tony. You do not want to be caught dreaming when that guy is around! Not that it helped too much to be focused, because Arsenal took it upon themselves to hand out an annual hammering. They were formidable, and if we escaped with a 4–1 defeat, then we were pleased to have at least scored, it was that bad.

But it was in that second game against United that I think I came of age, and I told myself that I'd arrived. I sat down before the game and said to myself 'Are you going to sit back and admire this lot, or are you actually going to show them that you can play yourself?' It was a case of coming out with, 'Hi, I'm here, everybody' but going on from there and doing something that would get people sitting up and taking notice. Brighty helped: he would say to me before matches, 'Ian, they're scared of you. No matter who they are, they are scared of what you can do to them. Don't disappoint them, do something special.' That was the biggest boost that anybody could have given me.

I scored my first ever goal in the top flight against United to get us a draw after Robbo had put them ahead. I'll always remember it: Alan Pardew played a great ball off the outside of his foot and I just chested it ahead of Mike Duxbury and got a foot to it. The relief was incredible and I just ran to the bench to celebrate my arrival. I've still got the boot I scored with in my trophy room at home and it's one of my proudest possessions.

We weren't kidding ourselves that Palace were going to win everything in sight, the players were realistic enough to know that it would be testing enough just to survive in Division One and prove that we were good footballers who could compete with some of the best in the country. Steve Coppell wasn't expecting too much either. He had been one of the best players of his generation, he knew that 90 per cent of the clubs in Division One didn't have a chance of winning the title. Even when he was at his peak with Manchester United and in a side that had six or seven stars, they didn't really get close to the Championship. All he told us was to play to our potential and we wouldn't discredit ourselves.

Steve may have been a flair player for United and England, but he wasn't under any illusions over how Palace should play. He knew that he had two players up front that could score goals against any side in the country, no problem, so he geared the team to play to our strengths. That meant getting the ball forward quickly and directly to let me use my pace to get behind defences, or getting the ball wide for the wingers to get crosses into the box for Brighty and then filling the opposition penalty area as quickly as possible. What he didn't want was any unecessary time on the ball that would allow opponents to regain possession and get at our defence.

It wasn't pretty, but 75 per cent of the time it was very effective. The boss didn't care about winning any style points, he just wanted real points, and enough of them in the bag to make sure we stayed up. Some of the players were fed up with the long-ball, route one approach, Brighty amongst them. He'd go in to Steve and say, 'Boss, we've really got to play a bit more football.' The answer would always be the same, 'How many goals have you got?' 'Twenty odd'. 'How many goals has Ian got?' 'Twenty odd'. 'So why do you want to change it?' And Brighty would come away having lost again. Steve's argument was that if the papers didn't like the way we played, who gave a damn? Journalists weren't going to give us the points to survive, so why should they dictate the way we went about things? I admired his determination and ruthlessness at sticking to what he thought was best even when we were getting criticised.

It was around this time that I first met my wife, Deborah. We'd known each other for a long time because we'd grown up on the same estate, Honor Oak, in Brockley, but we'd never really got talking. She's a few years younger than me and I wasn't really interested in younger girls at the time: I was a bit of a boy about town, going out with older women. But we'd always say hello to each other and I'd go to parties she attended with her mates, so we kind of kept up a nodding relationship.

I got to know her better after I smashed my car up and got banned for driving for six months. To cut a long story short, I tried to overtake a taxi, he didn't want to let me get by, and I ended up smashing into another car and getting a ban. I had to get a bus and then a train into training and I always seemed to be on the same bus as Deborah, and slowly we got talking to each other and getting along really well. She was good-looking, intelligent and was one of the most interesting people I had ever met. She wasn't like a typical south London girl who kind of drifts along through school and into a job for the rest of her life: 'Deb' was really strong-minded and knew exactly what she wanted out of life and I admired that.

We began to go out on a regular basis, for meals and to parties and I think we began to fall in love. At the time, I'd just split up with a girl and I was looking for commitment, not something that was going to be over in a few months. It may sound selfish but I was looking for somebody who would love me instantly, not grow to love me over the months. I wanted somebody who could accept me as just Ian Wright, not Ian Wright the footballer, and it seemed that Deb could do that. She had known me for years, she knew my background and what sort of person I was, so it seemed like a natural thing. I can honestly say that she is my life, and I have never regretted for one second having met her. I suppose it's the best thing a taxi driver has ever done for me, helping us to get together by running me off the road! I knew that Deb and I were meant for each other when she went on holiday to America. I have never missed anybody so badly as I did her while she was away, and as soon as she got back I knew I had to make sure she never left again, and we got engaged.

Thank God I had somebody's shoulder to cry on during the night of 12 September 1989, which will go down as one of the most humiliating times of my life. Wherever I end up when my career is over, I will never forget that night at Anfield when we lost 9–0 to Liverpool. I know what my idea of heaven is and it's a place where nobody will ever mention that game again or show a video of the goals or even mention the words 'Nine–Nil' for the rest of eternity. Even now I find it hard to put into words just how bad that game was. It was the Christians being thrown to the lions in Roman times and just walking up to the lions and putting their heads into their mouths. You would not believe how awful we were, how naive and how helpless we all felt as Liverpool just tore us apart. Make no mistake, they were bloody good that night and I had a grudging admiration for them, but that's no consolation when I remember the pain I felt.

We went to Anfield and ran around like headless chickens. We were three down at half-time – and it might have been six – but we said in the dressing room that if we got one back it would be a different game. Whom were we kidding? They just knocked the ball about, got another two, then another, then another and another. When the ninth went in, the tears of frustration were just rolling down my face – I couldn't stop them – because I was virtually a spectator for the whole ninety minutes.

At half-time, Steve said, 'You're going to have to screw your nuts on or this could be a very painful lesson. You have to work hard for each other.' We did work hard, but mentally we were just unable to cope with Liverpool. Physically we were fine, but they always seemed to be two thoughts and three yards ahead of us, no matter how hard or fast we ran. We just didn't know what was happening. I think at the end of the game they got changed and got back into the space-ship and went back to the different planet they'd come from, they were that good.

The next day I didn't even want to go out and show my face. Even when I did go out, people were laughing and mocking us. It is something that I will never ever forget because I never had the chance as a Palace player to get revenge on Liverpool. The other boys were in the side that beat them in the FA Cup semi-final, but I'd broken my leg and had to watch from the touchline, so it's something that will always stick with me and haunt me until my dying day.

The major casualty from that match was our goalie, Perry Suckling. My heart went out to him because he's a lovely guy and a really bubbly character, but that match was a disaster for him. Only a couple of weeks later, the club went and bought Nigel Martyn, the first £1 million goalkeeper, and that was the end of Perry who was eased out soon after. It was a really sad state of affairs because he never got a chance to wipe out that memory either.

Liverpool were really my bogey side that season because it was against them that I broke my leg for the first time. It was at Selhurst Park, the game was goalless, and I found myself clear through on Bruce Grobbelaar. I thought, 'Yes, you beauty, this is for the 9–0', when suddenly Barry Venison came across with a brilliant covering tackle. As he challenged me, my toe got stuck in the pitch and his left foot came through and hit me just above the ankle.

It felt bad but I thought it was just a twist, so I got up to run it off but I couldn't move or put any weight on it. Then I thought it was my ligaments, so I lay down and waited for our physio, Dave West, to come on with a stretcher. He said, 'Where does it hurt?' and I pointed to my leg. He touched it and – Jesus Christ! – I was like a cat going for the ceiling. I was in agony, and all Dave could say was that it looked like a broken fibula. So I was carted off to hospital, and he was right, the fibula was cracked.

By this time we were well into our FA Cup run which would eventually see us get to Wembley. We had beaten Portsmouth, Huddersfield and Rochdale pretty easily and were through to the quarter-finals where we had Cambridge away. That game was the target for me to get back for in six weeks. Everybody said it was impossible, that I shouldn't push myself too much or I could put myself out for the whole season. But I wasn't listening to them – all I wanted to do was get back and start playing because I had a feeling that this was going to be our season in the FA Cup, I felt that we were destined to get to Wembley, that God had ordered it.

It was a real slog, and I have never worked as hard as I did to get my fitness back. Dave West told me to take it easy, not to put too much strain on the leg, but I thought I knew best and I just went for it like a crazy man. The only time when I wasn't going through agony to get back playing was the day Deborah and I got engaged. I tell her the only reason she managed to trap me was because I had my leg in plaster, and there was no way I could hobble away quickly enough!

I don't know how I did it, but I convinced Dave and Steve Coppell that I was fit enough to play against Cambridge just six weeks after I broke my leg. But while the outside world thought I was ready, inside I knew that I'd come back too quickly. I couldn't feel anything when I ran or kicked the ball, but mentally I was not right. Whenever a defender came near me, I was terrified that something would happen again to the leg. And in hindsight, I now know I wasn't physically ready either. I got through the Cambridge game and we won 1–0, thanks to a Geoff Thomas goal and that set us up for a semi-final with Liverpool at Villa Park in April. Up to then, Steve said, he would nurse me through the matches: I wouldn't play in all of them, just enough games to get my match fitness back. The following Wednesday after beating Cambridge we were playing Derby and he put me in the side for that game.

Now I wish I had never clapped eyes on Derby or Paul Blades. I had done all right during the match, and when the ball came up to me and I got away from him, I didn't think anything of it. But then I felt the tackle; he couldn't have caught me in a worse place, exactly on the spot where the break had mended and just below. I was in absolute agony and Dave didn't have to tell me that the leg had broken again, but this time it was worse because it was a double break.

I'm not saying I came back too early because that would be unfair to Dave who I think, along with Gary Lewin at Arsenal, is the best physio I have ever worked with. If he said I was fit, then I was fit and ready to play. But to get hit on exactly the same spot is just a freak thing and although the bone should be strong enough to take it, sometimes you can't do a thing about it.

When the leg broke again, I thought my season was over. If I could get back with a few games to go, that would be a bonus, but I had virtually written the season off. It worked out that the time it would take to heal would take us to the week of the FA Cup Final, but to me that was no real incentive because the boys still had to get past Liverpool. But Dave West decided that he wasn't going to let me slip out of it that easily. He constantly drummed it into me that I could be fit for the final if I wanted to, and if Palace got there I would never forgive myself if I wasn't ready. He put me through the most rigorous fitness routine anybody has ever known and all the time he'd be drumming it into me, 'You've got to be ready for the final. You've got to push yourself for the final.' When I was on the exercise bike or doing my sit-ups, Dave would be there in my face, telling me how brilliant it would be to play at Wembley and what I would be missing if I didn't buckle down to it. Mentally he was preparing me for the final even though I didn't know it.

But the boys still had to beat Liverpool, and that day will go down as the most harrowing ever. How I didn't keel over from a heart attack even before the game started I will never know. I didn't travel up with the team on the bus: instead I went up with my mate Stuart Day and Mitchell Thomas. The traffic was absolutely dreadful and we got to Villa Park late, and it was only then that I realised I didn't have a ticket. There I was pushing through the crowds with my crutches, desperate to get in to see the lads in the dressing room and wish them luck.

What always happens when you're in that sort of situation? You run up against some imbecile in a uniform who does his best to win the Jobsworth of the Year title. This time it was the Brummie steward on the main entrance who wouldn't let me in without a ticket. I just had to see the boys' faces before the game, because that would tell me whether they had put the 9–0 disaster behind them and whether we could actually win it. I begged and pleaded with the guy and would have even gone down on bended knee except my leg was in plaster. Then I started to get angry and I swear to God I was going to chin him because he didn't care who I was, he wasn't going to let anybody through that door unless they had a ticket. I was going to whack him with my crutch and then try and run for it, until some kid came up with a programme and asked if I would sign it. I grabbed the prog-ramme and stuffed it under the steward's nose and screamed, 'Look, that's me, now let me in, you bastard.' That seemed to make the point, and his mate on the door gave me the OK and I was in.

I walked out of the tunnel and down the touchline and the fans started chanting my name. Then when the game started I felt sick in the pit of my stomach. I knew this was the biggest game Palace had ever played and I couldn't do a thing to help the boys. I don't think I've ever cried so much in the space of ninety minutes as I did during that match. Most people know that I'm an emotional person and that tears come pretty easily to me – sad films, happy films, you name it and I can cry because of it – but this was different, this was virtually one long bawling session.

I started when Brighty equalised Ian Rush's goal, I wept again when Gary O'Reilly put us ahead and I was still crying when Steve McMahon smacked one in a minute or so later. The tears turned to despair when John Barnes put Liverpool ahead, but then I went into overdrive as Andy Gray made it 3–3. Even before Alan Pardew got on the end of Andy Thorn's flick at the near post I was absolutely out on my feet, emotionally drained, but when Super Al's header went past Grobbelaar, I just could not stop myself. The broken leg was forgotten and I was dancing in delight, hugging Steve Coppell and anybody else I could get close to. I hardly heard the final whistle, but when I saw Palace fans streaming onto the pitch, I just lost it. I ran to meet Brighty, Andy and the lads, and everything became a blur. Just to see them so happy made me cry for about the fourth time and this time there was no way I could stop.

I owe a debt to Alan Pardew. Not just because he scored the goal that took us to Wembley, but for something he said a couple of years later. He said that I never gave enough credit to the other Palace players for helping me enjoy so much success in football, and he's right. It's only now, sitting down to do this book, that I realise what I owe those Palace boys, how much we all meant to each other and how good those times were. So, Al, if you ever read this, you were right, and I realise now just what you meant.

The FA Cup Final to me has always been the biggest game ever, bigger than World Cups or European Cups: it's the ultimate, and now I had the chance to play in it. Now all the pain and the running and the slogging my guts out with Dave West meant something because now I knew, without being big-headed, that if I proved myself to Steve Coppell, I had a chance of being there even if it was on the bench. I had a feeling that the boss wouldn't throw me straight into the side – he would stick with the one that beat Liverpool, and that was only right, so I resigned myself to a place on the subs' bench right from the start. I had no problem with that because, if I was to play, it would have disrupted the whole formation that had seen off Liverpool, and the boss wasn't about to do that, and rightly so.

It's difficult to describe what the FA Cup Final meant to me, just knowing that I was going to be involved. When I was a kid, I lived for the final, it used to be on television from 11 o'clock in the morning, and I'd be sitting in front of the TV until six that night: I would not move. The build-up was brilliant, with 'FA Cup Final Mastermind' or 'It's a Knockout', and then the cameras would go to the team hotels and do interviews there and on the bus – it was a brilliant, special day.

The first one I really remember was in 1972 when Leeds beat Arsenal, and Allan Clarke scored with a diving header and Mick Jones dislocated his shoulder. But the best I ever saw was when Arsenal beat Manchester United in 1979, and me and my mate Conrad were really into it. I lived in one block of flats and he lived in the opposite block a couple of floors above ours. We had to choose who we wanted to win, and I took Arsenal, and we agreed that each time either of our sides scored we would come out onto the balcony and shout insults at each other. So when Arsenal went 2–0 up I ran along the balcony shouting at the top of my voice and Conrad had to stand there and take it. But suddenly United started to come back. Gordon McQueen scored and Conrad went wild, then Sammy McIlroy got another one back and I just had to stand there in shame while Conrad ran amok. Fortunately, I got my own back when Alan Sunderland got the winner for Arsenal in the last minute, but by that time *everybody* was coming out on to the balcony to see what was going on and to find out who was making all the noise. They couldn't believe it was just kids enjoying a football match – they thought murder was being committed!

If I had only one medal from my whole career and it was an FA Cup winner's medal, then I would be happy to look back and say I had a great time as a footballer. When I think of all the great players who never played in a final, let alone won a medal, then it makes me proud to say that I have had the experience and have been fortunate enough to be there twice.

The week before Wembley was incredible. You get caught up in a whirlwind: everybody wants to know you, people are asking for tickets, you're doing television, radio, newspaper interviews, and you almost forget about the little things like training and preparation! I think we were lucky at Palace because the agent, Eric Hall, got involved. Now a lot of people don't like Eric, but he's never done anything wrong by me so I'm not going to get involved in criticising him. In fact he was brilliant: he helped the lads to relax because he was always a target for jokes and didn't care as long as he was making money. We made a few bob out of the players' pool, but I know something – he made a hell of a lot more! Some of the stunts he pulled were outrageous, just to earn another couple of quid, but all you could do was laugh at him because he pulled it off.

I have to say I sold my soul over a boot deal. I had worn Diadora boots all the way through the season and I liked them, they were comfortable and felt right for my feet. But Hi-Tech were offering all the lads a ridiculous amount of money for us all to wear their boots in the final, and everybody apart from Andy Gray was going for it. I didn't really know what to do but I came under a lot of pressure from the lads to wear them and, in the end, I went for it. Ron Silver, the guy who looked after me at Diadora, went absolutely mental, and I can't blame him. But Ron, in my defence, I was young and I got badgered by the lads, and if it's any consolation, I thought the Hi-Tech boots were so bad I got a pair of Mizunos, blacked out the bottoms and put the Hi-Tech stripes on them. That might not make Ron feel any better and I apologise now for scoring two goals!

The day of the final was everything I dreamed it would be. I had known from early on in the week that I was going to be on the bench because the boss wanted to play Brighty up front on his own with John Salako and Phil Barber wide, just as he had against Liverpool. But I didn't do anything different than I would have if I was starting: I did the warm-up, went out for the kick-in, shook hands with all the dignitaries and then slipped over to the bench.

The match seemed to pass by in a blur, and even though I've watched it hundreds of times on video I can't really remember too many incidents. Gary O'Reilly scored to put us in the lead, but Bryan Robson and Mark Hughes put United in front, and I have to admit that I thought it might be beyond us to get back. I remember thinking, 'Just give me ten minutes and I'll do something,' but as time slipped away it looked less likely that we could get anything from the game.

Then with twenty minutes to go, Steve told me to warm up. I was stretching down the touchline when he called me over and told me I was going on instead of Phil Barber. He said something like, 'Just go on and do anything you like to spark something, try and make a difference.' I can only remember vaguely what he said because I was thinking that if I got the ball anywhere near goal I was just going to shoot, never mind what anybody else thought.

The ball went out of play and I was on. I was trying to get into the game, but I couldn't get a touch of the ball, when suddenly Richard Shaw and Brian McClair challenged and the ball broke loose to Bright who flicked it into my path. I was already thinking, 'Get half a yard' when Mike Phelan came across to try and slide tackle me, so I knocked the ball past him.

Suddenly I'm in on goal but Gary Pallister was the covering defender. To this day, I always tell 'Pally' that he made me, that he helped put my name in lights, and I'll never let him forget it. He came storming over and all I could think was that he was so big that he could never stop in time, so I cut inside and left him kind of flat-footed going the other way, and now I had got a clear shot. The only thing on my mind was to put the ball into the other corner, across Jim Leighton, and as soon as I shot I knew it was in. Whenever you see people score in a final, they don't actually say anything, they just make a noise of pure, unadulterated joy, a kind of roar that you can't put down on paper and make it sound like it does. I made that noise. From somewhere deep inside me it came into my mouth and I just screamed. The tears were coming down my face because I had made a difference on the greatest day of my life. I ran past John Salako but he caught me and I went down on the pitch and all of a sudden there were four or five people on top of me making the same noise.

I was buzzing then and when the game went into extra-time

I felt good, I felt as if we were onto something big. Geoff Thomas knocked a ball out to John Salako on the left wing, he cut back onto his right foot and played a ball into the far post. All I remember is coming in, meeting it on the volley and the ball bulging into the roof of the net. Then it was a case of 'What the hell is going on?' I didn't know how to celebrate, I just ran to John Pemberton and started hugging him. All I could think was that God had blessed me, and I knew my life was never going to be the same. There's a picture of me as United are taking the kick-off and I've got my head back, looking up and I'm crossing myself, and that, to me, sums up those few moments. I was just thanking God for giving me this opportunity.

Mark Hughes spoiled the day when he equalised seven minutes from the end. He killed us but he probably saved Alex Ferguson's job and catapulted United towards what they've achieved in recent seasons. Without that goal, 'Fergie' might have been gone and who knows where United would have been.

I can't begin to put into words just how badly we were hurt by that goal. We had seen everything snatched away from us with that goal, and when you consider that we were just seven minutes away from the greatest story of our lives, it leaves a huge wound. I saw the goal in slow motion: Nigel Martyn and Gary O'Reilly both trying to close 'Sparky' down and the ball going past them and into the net. I don't blame either Nigel or Gary but you can't help thinking what might have been if Nigel had let Gary deal with it – did Nigel need to come out and spread himself? He did what he thought was best, but when you look back you wonder about things like that.

For all the wisdom that Steve Coppell has and all the respect that I have for him, there's still a small part of me that cannot forgive him for not having me on from the start in the replay. I know he'll understand that because he knows how badly I took it when he told the players that he was going with the same team that started the final. Brighty took him aside and said that I should play but Steve told him he was looking at the wider picture and that he couldn't afford for me to do my leg again and miss the start of the next season. If that was the case, why the hell was I playing in Trinidad the following week with big fellas kicking lumps out of me?

Steve was wrong. I knew that the sort of buzz that I was on, the sort of euphoria I was feeling could – and would – have made a difference. I know that Pally and Steve Bruce were wary of me, that they knew I was a danger. Paul Ince told me that when United found out I wasn't in, they were truly relieved. All I needed was an hour, sixty minutes to run at them and score or set something up, not for selfish reasons but for the good of the team, because I think the rest of the boys wanted me out there.

We never did ourselves justice in the replay: Lee Martin scored and we lost. I've never watched the game again and I never want to because it brings back such bad memories.

It's no use talking about could haves and what might have beens, but apparently Steve had a meeting with Bobby Robson, and Robson told him that if I had started the second game, then he probably would have taken me to Italia 90. I don't know if Steve thought telling me that would give me a boost, but I can tell you something, I was not pleased to hear those words.

7

A Problem
with Racism

The first time I pulled on an England shirt should have been one of the proudest days of my life. Instead it was spoilt for me in a terrible way by racism. The great memories I have of that night are overshadowed by the fact that I was targeted for abuse just because I was black, and the most sickening thing for me was that it happened virtually in my own back yard at Millwall.

I had been called up for the England B team to play Yugoslavia at the old Den in December 1989, and I was so thrilled that all the hard work I had put in with Palace and the goals that I had scored were finally being recognised. It thrilled me to know that I was just a step away from the full squad, that I was on the verge of real recognition at international level.

It was a bitterly cold night, but all my family and friends were there at the Den and I was keyed up and ready to go out and show people that, yes, Ian Wright had what it took to be a player on the world stage, not just at the pinnacle of the English game. But the first time I touched the ball, I was booed purely because of the colour of my skin.

I was absolutely appalled. I know that at a place like Millwall I'm going to get a rough ride, because firstly the fans fear me and want to do anything to put me off my game, and secondly I get will get racial abuse from a minority because at Millwall there is a problem with racism and there has been for as long as I can remember. But this was different, this was Ian Wright playing for England getting slaughtered because I was black, no other reason. I can generally handle racial abuse, but this time it hit me hard and, although it wasn't the only reason, I was pulled off at half-time and I left the Den feeling kicked in the teeth when really I should have walked away from there feeling sky high.

So much has been made of my feelings towards Millwall, but I swear I don't have a problem with the place or the fans – at least 95 per cent of them, anyway. How could I feel hatred against the club which I used to support as a kid? I remember I used to sneak into the Den with my mate Patrick when we were just in our early teens. The Cold Blow Lane End of the old Den in New Cross was less than a mile or so away from where we lived, and we used to go down there when Millwall were at home, climb onto a wall at the back of the stand and wait for the all clear. When there were no policemen about, we'd jump in and then watch the game for nothing.

I used to love those Saturday afternoons. Any opposition player will tell you that Millwall is the worst place in the world to go because at the old Den you were so close to the fans and you could hear every spit and snarl, and those boys could hand it out when they wanted to. But for the Millwall players it must have been like going into a coliseum as conquering heroes. To me, people like Barry Kitchener were giants, gods who could do nothing wrong. My favourite was a guy called Dave Mehmet who would always come on as a substitute and score or set a goal up and the crowd loved him.

Millwall had a couple of black players at the time, Phil Walker and Trevor Lee, and I was glad that they were playing because I was worried that if the fans didn't have a target on the pitch, they would turn on the black boy on the terrace. The fans were a mixed-up bunch. They would give the opposing black players real violent racist abuse and then turn round to me and say 'Nothing personal mate, it's because he's one of their black bastards.' I couldn't figure it out, but in those days I accepted it. Now I suppose there are Millwall fans who slaughter me because I'm black and are saying the same thing to their own black fans – it just doesn't make sense.

But, as I said, I don't have a problem with Millwall fans on the whole. When I meet any in the street they don't come up and give it the eyeball, they just shout out, 'Millwall' and make some remark about what rubbish they think Arsenal are; they don't want to rip my head off and kick it down the road.

The real problem I had with Millwall came a couple of seasons ago before a big FA Cup tie at the New Den. I did a piece with the Arsenal ClubCall guy and he asked me if there was a different atmosphere at places like Millwall. I said that when you played at somewhere like the Parc des Princes or any other great ground, the atmosphere inspired you, but at Millwall the atmosphere is so different and aggressive that you just want to stuff it up the fans there. Then he asked me if I thought there was still a racial element at Millwall and I said that there was and that it was common knowledge. The next day it was blasted all over the papers, 'WRIGHT WANTS TO STUFF IT UP RACIST MILLWALL FANS.' I couldn't believe what I was reading, and neither could George Graham. He went mad, telling me how stupid I was to stoke things up before what was going to be a hard enough game. Then when I got to the ground, the Millwall fans were waiting for me, wanting to know why I said that, when I was a south London boy and was supposed to be a man of the people.

The atmosphere in the ground that day was as ugly as I've ever known. From the kick-in to the last second of the match, I was booed, abused and insulted by the Millwall fans every time I went near the ball. It didn't help that the papers poured petrol on the flames by carrying a quote from Millwall Chairman Reg Burr that referred to me as an 'ignorant fool', despite the fact that he had not listened to the ClubCall tape. The match finished 0–0 and I've never been so pleased to get away from a football ground in my life. The next day I tried to put it right in the newspapers, but what I said still got twisted and I suppose I will be a marked man in the eyes of Millwall fans for the rest of my career. All I had done was answer questions honestly. Let's make one thing clear: there is a problem at Millwall over race, but neither I nor any other black player I know, goes there thinking, 'Yeah, I'm going to go there and stick two fingers up to those racists.' You go there knowing that there's going to be a problem, but confident that you can rise above it.

I've had to live with racism all my life, despite the fact that south London is one of the biggest multi-cultural areas of Britain. As a kid it was always 'Nig Nog' or 'Sambo' or 'Wog' and as a small child you know that it's said to you because you're black, but somehow it doesn't seem to worry you. It's not until you get a few years older that these slurs really begin to niggle you. It's just small things, like when it's hot, people come up and say, 'Warm enough for you now?' as if you come from some tropical jungle and you should feel happy now that England has been blessed with some sunshine.

It's pathetic that race should be a talking point in this day and age; haven't we got enough problems without the colour of your skin being a reason for abuse? Ever since I was a child there have been problems where I grew up: blacks, whites and Asians all wanted to fight each other, but what for? When whole cities can be wiped out by natural disasters, why do we want to kill each other because we've got different skins or different cultures?

People tell me I'm a role model for the black community and I'm proud to be seen as that. But sometimes I wish the black community would have a bit of pride in itself and see that there are greater things it can achieve. Slavery may have been abolished but a lot of black people are still living in mental slavery. It doesn't matter how high a black lawyer, doctor or even sportsman has gone in his profession, if he's the only black face in a room, he still feels like the little jumped-on nigger. You can't blame white people for that all the time because there are just as many bad black people as there are white; it's a case of self-pride and self-worth. We have to break free of those bonds. As Bob Marley put it, we have to emancipate ourselves.

As black people we also have to have pride in ourselves as a community. Men like Malcolm X and Martin Luther King gave us that pride, but who killed Malcolm X? A black person, and that is the worst point you can make. Bob Marley once said: 'Why must we keep killing our prophets?' And he was absolutely right. We have to rediscover that pride in ourselves first, and only then will we be able to move forward.

Martin Luther King was one of the greatest black men in history, and if he had been given the chance, he could have led us to equality. The first time I heard his 'I Have a Dream' speech, I broke down because it was so inspiring, and the way King preached was incredible – he set something alight in my heart. But although I admired him, I couldn't get my head around his passive protest style and the 'We shall overcome' attitude. It's all very well drinking from the cup of peace, but when that cup is being used to smash your head in, why should you turn the other cheek? Malcolm X said we should combat racism by any means necessary. That doesn't mean rushing out and shooting the first white guy that comes along, but it does mean using some force. It also means trying to compete in business, in politics and in every aspect of life.

I think we need a Malcolm X type figure these days. Not the Malcolm X who joined the Nation of Islam and preached separatism, but the Malcolm X after he went to Mecca and announced that we should sit round the table of brotherhood – black, white, yellow, brown – and just be able to talk on equal terms and be able to talk about hope. It's very easy for me to sit here, as a highly paid, highly recognised footballer, and preach, especially when I've never had it as bad as the players of the generation before me. My heroes were always Laurie Cunningham and Cyrille Regis, not just because they were exciting to watch and gave me a buzz whenever they got the ball, but because of what they had to suffer from the terraces. What we, as black players today, get is absolutely nothing compared to what Laurie, Big C and Viv Anderson had to go through. Then it was almost constant abuse at every ground that they visited, and they were more isolated because there were far fewer black players around in the 1970s and 80s.

I'm ashamed to say that I was a racist where Viv was concerned. It hurts me to say now because Viv is a friend who I really admire, but when I was young and ignorant I thought he was a 'coconut': brown on the outside but white inside. That's a terrible confession to make, but I thought he should have been doing more for the black players, not becoming part of the establishment. Now I know he was getting through it the best way that he could, and I know, because I've been on holiday with him, that he has as much pride in black people as anybody, he just expresses it in a different way. He was a man who did a great deal for black players in this country because he was the first black England international, just as when Paul Ince was the first black England captain. It may have been a small step for them but it was a huge leap forward for black footballers.

Football has still got to put its house in order. I'm sick to death of the trendy campaigns that seem to come around once every season, are in the spotlight for five minutes and still nothing changes. Last season I was criticised for not giving my full support to a campaign, but then a fortnight later Arsenal played Barnsley in the Coca-Cola Cup and Glenn Helder and I were booed from start to finish, not just by a handful of Barnsley supporters, but by virtually a whole stand. Their chairman apologised after the Commission for Racial Equality made a complaint, and the Arsenal vice-chairman, David Dein, sent him a letter on the club's behalf. But how on earth is a trendy campaign going to stop such ingrained hatred? I don't pretend to know the answer, but putting posters up and waving banners around isn't going to do the trick.

In its way, the subject of racism played a part in me leaving Crystal Palace. In 1991 a television company made a programme on race in football and asked Ron Noades for his comments. Now I respect and think very highly of Ron and he did a hell of a lot for me, but if you give him a soapbox, he will talk and talk and talk until he's talked himself into a corner. They put a camera and mike in front of him and what he said made pretty disgusting reading when it was reported in the *Sun* and the *Daily Mirror*. Basically, he said that black players were fine if you wanted flicks and fancy footwork, but when the weather got cold and there was frost on the ground, then you needed some good old white heart and spirit to see a team through. I didn't know what the hell was going on or why he had said it when there were six black players in the Palace side at the time and we had just been to an FA Cup Final after having our best ever season in the top flight. It seemed like a dreadful slur.

Later, I found out that he'd said a lot more that was complimentary to black players, but those comments were edited out and only the bad things left in. At the time, I reacted in a natural way and I reported him to the Commission for Racial Equality. I felt under a lot of pressure because people saw me as a figurehead at Palace for the black players and for my community. They were waiting to see what I would do, and if I had just sat back and done nothing, then I know what they would have been saying. It would be: 'That Ian Wright's done nothing when push came to shove' and I would have been viewed as a white man's puppet by the black community. I come from a black area, along with Andy Gray, and because I'm from that kind of background, I had to stand up and be counted when the chips were down. I couldn't let it go, I couldn't let it be seen that a white man could benefit from a black man but then turn round and dump on him at the first opportunity. In hindsight, I may have overreacted, but at the time I had to do what I thought was the right thing. That incident broke a lot of bridges between me and Palace that I don't think were ever mended, although my relationship with Ron hasn't changed, thank God. He knows he said some stupid things and I know a lot of what he said was ignored, so there are no hard feelings and I will always respect him for the help that he gave me as a player and the advice he still gives me.

8

The Gunners and
the Golden Boot

In my last full season with Palace, I started looking around at
players at other clubs and I began to ask myself questions. I
wondered whether I could cut it with a bigger club on a bigger
stage and whether I had what it took to become one of the top
players in the country, not just a big name in London. As soon
as that happens, if you're ambitious, then it's only a question
of time before that itch becomes so bad that you have to get
away.

I felt so much for Palace that I really had a feeling of dis-
loyalty just having those thoughts, but then I realised that I
owed it to myself to try and be the best I possibly could and
I didn't think that I could do it at Palace. For a long while in
that 1990/91 season I thought it might just be possible that
Palace could help me fulfil my ambitions because that was
the season that everything really clicked for us as a side.

Suddenly people feared us. We'd pushed Manchester
United all the way in the FA Cup Final, we'd given Alex
Ferguson the fright of his life with our first performance at
Wembley and, looking at us, we had a team that meant busi-
ness. Brighty and I were probably one of the best striking
partnerships around, perhaps the best when you look at our
scoring records over the four seasons that we played together.
We had a great midfield with Geoff and Andy as well as John

Salako, and our defence was probably one of the toughest to break down, especially with Nigel Martyn in goal.

Steve had perfected a system that wasn't always pretty to watch, but it frightened the life out of teams and got results, good results as well. If the Cup Final season had seen Palace come of age, the next year we matured into one of the top sides in the country. You don't have to take my word for it – talk to any of the sides we turned over along the way. We weren't afraid of anybody and, even though we didn't think we could win the title, we knew we could finish in the top five or six, we had that much belief in ourselves.

But still there was always that feeling in the back of my mind that there had to be something else. There were constant rumours in the papers that this club and that club were in for me, that Palace would listen to anybody who put £2 million on the table including Liverpool, Manchester United, Spurs and Arsenal. Then there were rumours that a couple of Spanish clubs were interested and that a team in Italy had been watching me. It was flattering, but it was also distracting. I had journalists asking me when I was going, other players were saying that they'd heard things on the grapevine, and every time I went out there were Palace fans begging me not to go. Even the Palace boys were beginning to ask questions because they had heard the rumours and they wanted to know exactly what was going one, but I couldn't answer them. Of course I wanted to know where my future was going to be, but the way Palace were playing that season, I wasn't going to rock the boat.

We were going like a train. At Christmas we were right up there with the leaders and going to places like Old Trafford and Anfield and Goodison Park and coming away with something. And against the likes of Wimbledon and Coventry and QPR we were dishing out the punishment, with really great performances that made the critics sit up and take notice of us and believe we could be title contenders.

We eventually finished third that season which was absolutely incredible considering the size of the club and our limited resources. It was a great testament to the players that were there at the time and to the spirit that we had. There was not one weak link, not one moaner or whiner, and no cheats, which hardly any other side in the country could, hand on heart, say about themselves. The fans that year were magnificent as well, following us all round the country irrespective of the weather conditions, and I felt good about giving them something to cheer about as well.

We also went back to Wembley in the final of the Zenith Data Systems Trophy and finally won there. We didn't just win, we battered Everton both in a footballing way and a physical way. They went away whinging that we'd been like bullies in the playground, but we went away with winners' medals and for me that cancelled out all the criticism that anybody threw at us. I finally had a medal and I'd been a winner at Wembley, and suddenly it dawned on me that I liked the feeling, that I wanted more of it: in fact I wanted it all the time. I needed to be winning things, I needed to see my trophy room full up with silverware and mementos and everything else that went with being a winner. But I also realised that it wasn't going to be with Palace.

We finished third that year and the club should have built on that success and tried to go a step further. Instead, Palace sat back, thought how wonderful it had all been, what a brilliant time it was and let everything that we had built up slip through its fingers. We finished third and Leeds finished fourth. During the summer they went out and bought Tony Dorigo and Rod Wallace, not the biggest or most glamorous names in the world, but two good players who could strengthen their side, make competition for places and add something to Leeds. What did Palace do? Nothing. What happened? Leeds went out and won the Championship and we started the season as if everything the year before had meant nothing and a nice comfortable mid-table position would be fine. That's when I realised that Palace lacked the ambition that I had and that if I was going to enjoy more and more success, it would have to be away from Selhurst Park. How could I hold my head up with the likes of Tony Adams when he had won everything going and all I had to point at was a Zenith Data medal?

The first few weeks of the 1991/92 season went okay: I was scoring regularly and the team were doing fine but I have to say I wasn't really enjoying it. I knew there had been interest from Arsenal, and Spurs were also in the background, and basically I just began to get impatient and made it known to both Steve Coppell and Ron Noades that I wanted to get away. They both knew what the score was; they knew the day was fast approaching when they wouldn't be able to stand in my way because somebody was going to make an offer that Palace just could not refuse. Two million pounds is a hell of a lot of dough to a club like Palace; it may not sound much four years later, but at the time it was a massive amount. Besides, they had also made plans for my replacement. Stan Collymore had come down from Stafford Rangers and I think that they were grooming him to play alongside Brighty when I left.

I want to put the record straight as far as Stan is concerned. Alan Smith, who was Steve's assistant at the time before taking over as manager, has said that it was the players who forced Stan out of Palace, and that it was especially me and Brighty giving him stick. That, as far as I'm concerned, is totally untrue. The main people giving Stan a hard time were 'Smithy' and Wally Downes, one of the coaches at the time. Smithy didn't like Stan because he thought there were kids coming up from the youth team and reserves who had more skill and had a better attitude. Wally thought Stan was an easy target and was on his back every second of the day. Stan later chinned him, and I have to say I don't blame him one bit. I didn't have a problem with Stan. In fact I liked him, he was dead straight and quite funny in his own way. After I left Palace I know Brighty fell out with him, but that was weeks after I'd joined Arsenal.

When the move did finally happen, it went through so quickly that I couldn't believe it. It was the middle of September and we played Oldham on the Saturday at their place and I scored along with Brighty and John. On the Sunday, I went round to see Ron Noades at his home, as I often did, just to have a chat. He was in the middle of a dinner party but popped out to see me. I didn't stay long, just long enough to tell him that I knew Arsenal were very interested and that I hoped that even though I had a couple of years left on my contract, he wouldn't stand in my way. I knew I could talk to Ron like that, knew he would respect me being straight with him. He didn't really say anything and I left.

The next day I went into training really fired up. I was going to storm in to see Steve and tell him that if he or Noades tried to stop me leaving I'd play up, I'd make a nuisance of myself and make it so unbearable for everybody that they'd have to let me go. Instead, Steve pulled me over before training started and said, 'You've got to go and speak to Arsenal, the club have accepted a bid.' I went from having all the front in the world, ready to give it the big time, to a scared little kid terrified that a club like Arsenal wanted to speak to me, because Arsenal were always the club and the team I looked up to. They were everything I thought a big side should be: formidable, daunting and scared of nothing or nobody. Whenever we played at Highbury, I would just look at the sheer scale of the place and it would send a shiver through me – all that history and success made me feel so small. It was the same whenever they came to Selhurst Park. Tony Adams, Steve Bould, David Seaman and Paul Merson would walk through the door and I would think, 'Christ, they're here and they mean business.' Just to think that a club like that would be interested in me was enough to set the old fears going. Was I good enough? Could I fit in? Would I even get in the team? That was all racing through my mind as I set off to meet Arsenal and talk over a move that would change my life.

I was gearing myself up to meet George Graham, the manager, but he decided that he would rather play golf and left it all to the managing director, Ken Friar, to do all the negotiations. I thought at the time, 'Yeah, cheers, George. Thanks for being there when I had to make the biggest decision of my life.' But I've since found out that he was playing golf with some journalists and the fact that he knew while he was out there with all those press men that Arsenal were making their biggest ever signing, and didn't say anything, would have given him a buzz and I can appreciate that.

The deal had to be done in a hurry because I had to sign in time for me to make my debut at Leicester in the League Cup on the Wednesday. Everything was going smoothly and I was just ready to sign when a fax came through from Ron Noades. Basically it said that if I didn't relinquish all the signing-on fees that I was owed by Palace for the rest of my contract, the deal was off and I'd have to go back to Palace.

For once in his life, Ron summed me up wrong. He thought I was the type of player who was moving purely for financial reasons and would hang out for the very last penny that I was owed. He could not have been wider of the mark if he thought I was going to jeopardise a move to a great club like Arsenal just for the sake of a few quid I was owed. I was really disappointed that Ron should have done something like that; it was as if the relationship we had built up over the previous five or six years meant nothing to him. I turned to Ken Friar and said, 'Tell Ron he can stick his dough as far up his arse as he can, I'm not going back!' I've never been money motivated. I live by the words that my agent, Jerome

Anderson, told me way back in my early years with Palace. He said, 'If you do the business on the park, then everything else will come because it goes hand in hand.' That has always been my philosophy and that I will stick by.

I suppose it was only business, but I'm sorry now that my last dealings with Ron had to end on a sour note because, as I've said before, I respect him. A lot of people think that he's just a money-grabbing businessman who has no morals, but without him Palace would be nowhere. He has grabbed every opportunity that he can, he has a great eye for the future and he's the main man at Palace, make no mistake about that. I don't think anybody connected with the club should have any illusions: without Noades, there might not be a Palace.

Ron and Steve were the two main reasons that I became such a success at Palace. Steve put me on the stage, he gave me the chance and I will never be able to thank him enough for what he did for me. He saw something in the cocky little kid who came along for a trial, and gave me the opportunity to fulfil my dream. I've had a few managers in my time, but nobody has ever been so honest with me. If he thought I'd played well, he'd always tell me, and if he thought I'd been useless, then he would let me know. There are no grey areas with him: what you see is what you get, and if you don't like it, then tough. I owe him virtually everything.

It was hard leaving the Palace lads, especially Brighty. We were as close as any brothers and I'll always appreciate what he said when he heard I was going. It wasn't emotional or anything like that, he just said, 'Go for it, you deserve it.' That meant more than anything else, coming from someone whom I'll always admire and respect above any other player.

I put pen to paper with Arsenal about two hours after we sat down to talk and that was it: so easy yet such a massive step. I woke up on Monday morning a Crystal Palace player and went to bed an Arsenal player. There were no hassles, there was no auction with Palace trying to get in other bids, the deal was done and dusted and I was happy. No, in fact I was delighted!

Looking back, I now realise just what a massive step it was for me. At the time I got caught up in it, the thrill of the move and everything, I didn't realise what it would mean to my life. Now I can quite honestly say, if I never kicked a ball again, I could quit the game satisfied that I have achieved what I've achieved with one of the greatest teams in the world and nobody can ever take that away from me.

People outside Highbury just don't realise how good the club is. They think everything is just hard, aggressive and professional, but once you get inside the club you see that everybody concerned with the club is pulling for Arsenal. From the groundsman to the chairman, everybody has Arsenal carved on their hearts and they only want the best for it. That really struck me when we were going through the bad times two seasons ago. Instead of crying, moaning or whinging and giving it the self-pitying bit, everybody just pulled together and tried to shut it all out, as though we were absolutely determined not to let it affect us. That's the kind of club we are and once you've savoured that special kind of bond and commitment to the club, then you never want to lose it or leave it. Look at the backroom staff, the likes of Pat Rice, Geordie Armstrong and Bob Wilson: their lives are joined up in Arsenal and they love just being associated with it. When any player leaves Arsenal, you'll never hear them slaughtering it because after a while they realise that they'll never be treated as well anywhere else and they'll probably never be as successful.

It could have been very difficult for me to fit in, and now I praise God that I didn't dig my heels in with Palace and demand my money from Ron Noades, because that would have meant me missing the game against Leicester. I might not have scored on my debut and could have struggled, as a lot of strikers do when they join clubs, through not hitting the back of the net straight away. Thankfully I forgot about the dough and just tried to get on with my game.

What I couldn't forget was the price tag. Arsenal had busted their club record and shelled out £2.5 million on me, and I don't care what anybody says, when a big club splashes that sort of dough around on you, it frightens the life out of you! If you ever hear a player say, 'Well, I didn't set the price, so it doesn't bother me,' then they're lying through their teeth. Of course it bothers you, you're the one that's got to go out and justify it, you're the one that's got to put up with the mockery from the fans if you don't cut it straight away and you're the one who has to face up to the press and media questioning whether you're worth it.

So when I went out on to the pitch at Filbert Street in the League Cup two days later, the nerves were almost killing me. The Leicester fans were calling out 'What a waste of money!' and that was just piling on the pressure, putting that little bit of doubt in my mind, making me try too hard instead of doing the easy thing. It was a tough game as well: Leicester were right up for it, they were going to show us that they weren't going to be pushed around. Suddenly Colin Gibson tried to play the ball out of defence but it went straight to Paul Davis who played a blinding flick with the outside of his left foot right into my path as I was running towards the penalty area. I controlled the ball with my left foot, but as I was running, I slipped. I was still able to get up and I knew I just had to hit it across the keeper and into the far corner and it went in.

The relief was incredible: the sheer fact that I had done in my first match what Arsenal had bought me to do was such a high point for me that the goal will always be ingrained in my memory. And that's the thin line that you tread, the luck that you have to ride if you're a striker. Had I not scored in that game, then perhaps I would have been more anxious going into the next game, more nervous to get things right and it could just have gone the other way. The opportunity is there, the luck is there and you have to take it.

I can't really explain the way I felt about my league debut, it's just fairy-tale stuff. We played Southampton and I scored a hat-trick. I just could not believe this was happening to me. I felt on a high, but dazed at the same time, just thinking that it couldn't be possible, that things could not be going this right for me after just two games. George Graham came up to me after the game and told me that it was the best debut anybody has ever made for Arsenal. All I said was, 'Cheers, Boss', and it didn't really sink in to me at the time, but now I know about the history of the club and the great players they've had over the years, I realise just what an honour George was giving me.

The season just went on and on from there with goals coming almost at will. There were times when I'd come off the pitch hardly sweating but I'd scored twice. Two chances – BANG! BANG! – in the back of the net without me having to kill myself making this run and that run, trying to shake off defenders. That was down to the Arsenal lads because they were enjoying the scoring run as much as me, they were getting a thrill out of me going for the Golden Boot because it meant they were winning and picking up points.

Merse, Alan Smith and Kevin Campbell were incredible – they were just piling chances on a plate for me, and because I was hitting such a rich vein of form, they were going in without me knowing too much about it. But above every-body else, Anders Limpar was the boy doing the business for me, and I sorely missed him when he moved to Everton because at one stage he created 95 per cent of my goals. Ironically it was against Everton that I had my best scoring performance of the season when I got all our four goals, but to be fair, Anders was the star of the show that day. He put four chances on a plate. He was going to the goal-line and rolling it across for me to tap in, because he just seemed to enjoy setting up things for other people. I still scored the same ratio of goals when he left, but I had to work twice as hard to get them.

The whole season was just like a flight, it took off and kept going. I had the fans on my side straight away because I was scoring goals and they knew I could deliver the goods; they always felt I could pull the side out of the mire if things weren't looking good and I loved repaying that faith. But football fans are a strange breed: the more they love you the more the expectancy level rises. They always want more, more, more.

Last pre-season was a perfect example of that. I wasn't doing anything different from what I'd done before at Arsenal, but because we'd signed Dennis Bergkamp and David Platt the heat had been turned up just that extra notch and the fans were expecting miracles all the time. What I'd done over the last four years didn't mean anything to the fans: what they wanted was something extra. Whereas before if I'd flogged my guts out on a 20-yard run to get to a pass, they'd say 'Unlucky, Wrighty' and realise that I was working hard, last season it was, 'Shift your ass, Wright, come on,' and sometimes that's hard for a player to take. The Arsenal fans know that I will always try and work my hardest for them, but when you hear them telling you to get your finger out, then you sometimes have to wonder whether you really need it.

I'll give you a little insight into fans. Palace supporters will always be a huge part of my life and I used to love them, but now I feel the opposite way. When I first went back to Selhurst Park, they were brilliant: they clapped me and cheered my name at the end. But when they came over to Highbury, I was absolutely slaughtered. I went to pick up the ball for a throw-in and a little girl who couldn't have been more than about 12 years old shouted 'Judas' right in my face. Now you're not telling me she thought that one up all on her own – she'd heard it all through the game, plus a lot more besides. One lovely little ditty went, 'Ian Wright is illegitimate, he ain't got a birth certificate.' Now you have to wonder about the sort of minds that can make up that sort of rubbish.

I didn't score in that game but I made it my life's ambition to score against Palace no matter what, just because of the way the fans treated me. And supporters don't seem to realise just what a boost that sort of abuse gives players. It fires you up to such an extent that you just know you're going to play well. Arsenal supporters were the same last season with Kevin Campbell. Of course I wanted to beat Forest, but I was pleased for Kevin that he scored after the way our fans treated him. If fans boo afterwards, then you're not bothered: you can just point to the paper the next day and show them your name alongside one of the goals.

But in that first season, the Arsenal fans were brilliant and they were carrying me along with their desire and demands and I rose to it. I was head to head with Gary Lineker for the top goalscorer and to me that was a thrill all on its own: me right up there with The Man. He was leaving Spurs at the end of the season for Japan, going out on his white charger with the Player of the Year award in his hand and one eye on a knighthood – which, by the way, he deserves – and all he needed to crown it all was the Golden Boot.

We had a brilliant rivalry that season. We'd phone each other up after every match and wind each other up, but we knew that it was going right down to the wire. I'd score in a couple of games and he'd miss out, then I'd go two or three without scoring and he'd get a hat-trick or something so there was a real competitive streak and edge to the battle. It went right down to the last day of the season and that day, 2 May, will always stick in my mind. Gary was one ahead going into the game but Spurs were at Manchester United so I didn't fancy his chances, while we were at home against

Southampton. I don't know what it is about Southampton, but I always do well against them and always score goals, so I was well up for it. We came in 0–0 at half-time but somebody told me that Lineker had scored at Old Trafford, so it meant I needed a hat-trick to beat him.

It seemed like Mission Impossible but all the boys were behind me and desperate to set something up and with the fans willing me on I still felt as if I could do it. We got a penalty and Lee Dixon, who normally would have taken them, gave me the ball which was a brilliant thing to do, total class. I put that away and then it just seemed like a rollercoaster ride. Merse set me up for a second and then, with the seconds ticking away, I went through and got it, the third goal that beat Lineker and won me the Golden Boot.

He phoned me that night and just said, 'Congratulations, you deserve it.' That meant more to me than picking up the actual award because, in my mind, Lineker is the Master. He and Ian Rush are my heroes, the men who have been top of their trade for the last fifteen years, and the strikers whom I've modelled myself on. I wouldn't have minded losing the boot to Lineker, but sometimes I look at it in my trophy room and think to myself that it would have been at his house and that gives me a major buzz.

I have total respect for Gary and that's why I was disappointed when Nike put up the posters at the end of the season with 'Gary who?' on them. That wasn't right and I thought it was a mistake because it showed him complete disrespect. All right, it was a 'street cred' kind of thing, but at the end of the day it was wrong. When his sponsor, Quasar, retaliated with a dig at my England record, 'Lineker 48 Wright 0', I had to hold my hands up and agree with them. But going to the ceremony and picking up the Golden Boot award capped a brilliant season for me and I finally realised that I'd made it.

9
My England Career

I first really felt that I had a chance to be an England player during my Palace days. We'd got promotion and everybody knew that I'd scored a bagful of goals in a lower division, but then I showed that I could do it right at the very top. Bobby Robson gave me my first taste of England glory when he picked me in the B team at Millwall. That night may have been a sickener because of the abuse I got from the crowd, but just to play alongside people like Gazza, Tony Adams, David Batty and Mike Newell convinced me that this was a stage where I had to shine. That was the nearest I got under Robson, although I know he was looking at me as part of the squad to go to the World Cup Finals in 1990.

But the man who gave me my real chance was Graham Taylor. I'd got my move to Arsenal and had continued to score bundles of goals, so I don't think that he could ignore me. But as far as the way he treated me during his time as England manager, I think he would have quite happily never picked me except for the fact that most newspapers and television reporters were demanding that I should be given a chance.

I know he didn't appreciate the way I was, or my sense of humour, and I know that he tried to show me up and slap me down just to put me in my place. But Taylor hated the fact that I was an individual and didn't tug my forelock or agree with every single word that he said.

And I'll tell you what, he certainly had a few words. He may not ever have been good enough to play for England or even that good an England manager, but he certainly could *talk* for England. In fact he would have captained England for talking against the Rest of the World, no shadow of a doubt! That man would talk and talk and talk until the cows came home and then he'd continue talking until they were fast asleep.

The problem was, most of it didn't make any sense to me. Good managers or coaches say all they have to say shortly and sharply; if they go on for longer than ten minutes, they've lost it, because players will switch off. It's the same thing at school. If you really want to get into a subject – science or art or PE – you want to get into it right away, no hesitation. A few basic instructions from the teacher and then you're off, BANG! into it and enjoying it. If the teacher drones on and on, you feel like saying, 'Blow this, what's next? I'm bored out of my skull.'

My card was marked as early on as 1990. In one of the first squads Taylor called me into, we were all standing around in a circle with him in the middle. That was one of his favourite tricks; he'd be in the middle and Lawrie McMenemy would stand round the outside watching all the players that Taylor couldn't see.

Anyway, he'd been going on for about 25 minutes and he'd lost me and most of the others. It's not that I've got a short attention span, but I was bored rigid. All I wanted to do was get the balls out, get working and show him what I could do. Suddenly I glanced across at the other side of the circle and Tony Coton, the Manchester City goalie, was rolling his eyes in his head as if he was about to fall asleep and topple over. That was it, I got a fit of the giggles and had to do everything I could not to burst out laughing. I was nodding my head seriously with every point Taylor was making but inside I thought I was going to wet myself as I struggled not to laugh in his face. Taylor clocked me and I think from then on it was downhill all the way.

Our big falling out was on the England trip to Australia, New Zealand and Malaysia in the summer of 1991. Goals were just flooding in wherever we played and it was a striker's dream because the defences were poor and chances were coming left right and centre. It was the sort of set-up where Gary Lineker could have taken his sleeping bag onto the pitch, set it up on the 18-yard line, fallen asleep and still scored a hat-trick, it was that simple. But it got round to the match against Malaysia and I was on the bench. It was hot, sticky and my legs had fallen asleep. I got up to stretch them and Paul Parker said, quite innocently, 'Why don't you come and sit down?' I just said flippantly, 'F*** that, I'm not used to sitting on benches.' Taylor heard that and ignored me for the rest of the trip and didn't pick me again for another eighteen months.

That might sound a bit childish, but it soon got to be deadly serious between us when he did something that I consider unforgivable: leaving me out of the squad for the 1992 European Championships in Sweden. As far as I was concerned, it was a nightmare for me. I am a great believer in strikers having their time and, I tell you, that was my time without a doubt. I'd laid all the foundations, I'd signed for a big club for big money and I'd shown every single person in the country that I could cut it. I'd ended up winning the Golden Boot for being the top scorer, even beating Gary Lineker. Nobody can tell me that I didn't deserve a place on that plane to Sweden. Nobody will ever convince me that I wouldn't have made a difference for England in some of those matches.

Taylor tried to tell everybody that he couldn't take both Lineker and me. That's complete nonsense, the biggest load of rubbish I've ever heard! I wasn't going out to Sweden to replace Lineker, one of the greatest strikers the world has ever known: I was going out to be Ian Wright, the most successful centre forward in the country at the time, the man with the records to prove it.

All I was waiting for was the call-up to finish the season in a blaze of glory. But what did Taylor do? He picked Alan Shearer. Now I'm not having a go at Alan, but how did he deserve a shout ahead of me? Isn't he the same sort of player as Lineker? And how many goals had he scored that season? About half of what I'd scored.

This is the first time that I've ever spoken out about the situation. At the time, I didn't need to say anything because every newspaper in the country was saying it for me. Even journalists whom I hated and who hated me were asking questions and pointing fingers, demanding to know how Taylor could even think about leaving the top striker in the country out of the squad. This is not sour grapes, but it just has to be said. Taylor has got away with it for too long and I have to put my side of the story.

It took a long, long time to get over a disappointment that big, and I still think there's a part of me that hurts because I wasn't allowed to show what I could do when it was my time on the big stage. There's also the frustration that I could never show people how good I was in an England shirt. You still hear it now, 'Oh, Ian Wright's a great striker for Arsenal but he could never produce the goods for England,' and that cuts so deep.

One journalist wrote that I'm a good striker but not a great finisher at international level. That's a load of rubbish as well. There have been players who are far better than me who could not score for England to save their lives, and there are worse strikers who'll score buckets of goals. It all comes down to luck, and if that's on your side then you have a major advantage.

I never thought that I had luck on my side for England. I could have scored on my debut against Cameroon, and then who knows what might have been, but Gary Lineker stuck out his foot, deflected my shot in and that was that, another goal to the master, a blank for Wrighty. There's a great picture of me as the ball is crossing the line. I don't know whether to laugh or cry because England have scored, but I know Lineker had nicked a goal that was rightly mine. The line between being a success and not doing so well at international level is a very thin one, and if Gary hadn't poached that one then who knows what I would have done for my country.

I know I only had two bad games for England. One was against Norway in 1991 when I missed a couple of chances, and the other was against Russia the same year when I was marked so tightly I couldn't even breathe let alone score. The rest of the time I know that I've been at my best. I still watch the tapes even now and I can see that I worked hard and did some nice things which I know my team-mates appreciated, but because I haven't reproduced my Arsenal form, banging in hat-tricks left, right and centre, critics will say I have failed.

It also helps if you're asked to play in exactly the same way as you do for your club. Gary Lineker always told me, 'Keep doing what you're good at and things will work for you.' But how can I do what I'm good at for Arsenal when I was asked to do completely different things for England? I've played as a winger and been told to track full-backs into defence, I've played as the man coming from deep or the second striker, when all I've ever wanted to be is the main man. If it's good enough for Arsenal, then why can't it be good enough for England? All I ever wanted was to be up there as the spear-head with a winger getting balls into the box and then I know I'd get a nick or a touch and the goals would start flowing.

Taylor never had the slightest bit of faith in me. The only time I ever felt part of the England set-up was when I scored in Poland, in May 1993, to give us a draw in a World Cup qualifier when, surprise, surprise, I came off the bench. But what happened next match? I was back on the bench. I think in all the matches I played for England I only started two consecutive games, so how was I supposed to feel? I knew that Taylor didn't fancy me and was being forced to throw me on for ten or fifteen minutes, so I'd be so keyed up for that time that I wasn't myself. I wasn't relaxed and that hindered me.

Perhaps I made some mistakes with Taylor. Perhaps there was something in my attitude that made him think that he didn't have to have any regard for my feelings. Early on, he decided to drop me and took me to one side and tried to explain why I wasn't playing. I just said, 'Look, you're the England manager, you don't have to justify your decisions to me, I'm pleased just to be part of the squad.'

Perhaps he took me at my word and didn't think that I had the hunger and desire to be an England player. Because it seemed from then on it didn't matter how well I was playing for Arsenal or how many goals I was scoring, he just discarded me and brushed me away without giving any kind of explanation.

All I ever remember about my England career is coming on to try and rescue a match. It's always been, 'Get Wrighty on, he might do something.' It's a dreadful feeling knowing you're only seen as the ace up the sleeve, the rescue man. The worst time was against Holland 1994 when Dennis Bergkamp had scored and I was getting warmed up. Just as I was about to go on, Koeman put his free kick away and I thought to myself, 'Great, not only do I have to score once, I've got to get another and turn this game on its head.' That is not a nice feeling when there's only about twelve minutes left.

When I look back at that television programme about our World Cup qualifying matches, I can't feel sorry for Taylor – I'm too busy laughing! I feel sorry for Lawrie McMenemy because I think he realised just what kind of a nightmare the programme was going to be and seemed to distance himself as much as he could. But as for Taylor and his assistant Phil Neal – or should I call him 'Yes, Boss' – they got exactly what they deserved. They came out of it looking like the Three Stooges.

The whole thing was a joke from start to finish. When Taylor was trying to explain to Nigel Clough what he wanted when he went on as a substitute, it was complete gibberish, it did not make one word of sense. And in the game against Holland, Taylor had to be talking for the sake of the cameras when he was having a go at the linesman. You cannot tell me that anybody speaks like that in real life unless he's talking for a television audience back home.

It was a mistake from start to finish. If Taylor wanted to give an insight into what the England set-up was like behind the scenes, why not wait until we'd qualified for the World Cup and then it would have been glory, glory? Instead it made him look like a joke and made the FA the laughing stock of the country.

One thing I will say for Taylor, he told me that he would have taken me to the World Cup if England had qualified. I don't know what I would have been doing – cleaning boots or making the tea – but I would have been there!

When Terry Venables took over I thought that I might be in with a shout again. George Graham had always told me that Venables liked my attitude and my desire, and thought highly of me. I didn't know the man at all except to say hello to. In fact the longest conversation we'd ever had was in the toilets at Wembley after we'd beaten Spurs in the FA Cup semi-finals. He wished me luck and said that he admired the way that Arsenal had been gracious in victory, which was a hallmark of George – he never liked us to rub peoples' noses in it, even Tottenham's. Venables also told me he tried to buy me from Palace but Spurs didn't have the money.

As a manager I think he's probably one of the best: his record speaks for itself and his coaching ability is second to none. In all the time I played under Taylor, he never once coached me or did a real session on finishing. The first day under Venables, we were working on shooting almost straight away and he made some points that will stay with me. He made me feel good. He told me just to do the simple things, but do them well. It was always, 'Pass it and then get in the box,' or 'Find your man and make your run.'

To me this was all music to my ears because he was working on my strengths and trying to make me a better player, which I appreciated. He always wanted things done with a little bit of class and style. Even if it was just a simple ball, he insisted that we made the right shape and had a little bit of quality about ourselves and that was what I will always remember about Venables. I still carry that into my training now and keep trying to do everything with a little bit of class.

I was in his first couple of squads, but the Christmas Tree formation and I never really worked out. Against Romania I found myself stuck out on the left wing chasing Dan Petrescu whenever he decided to move forward, which was all the time as far as I can remember. Then after two or three squads, Venables called me up to say that I wasn't selected because he wanted to take a chance and have a look at a couple of others. I told him I appreciated the call, because he didn't have to ring and explain things, and wished him all the best for the match. I put the phone down and for about twenty seconds I was just cold inside because I had the feeling that was the end of my England career. I just stared into space and then I said to myself 'To hell with it, just get on with your life.'

And I've had to get on with my life, but I will never get over the fact that I'm not going to get that buzz ever again. When you find out that you're in the squad, no matter how many you've been in, that buzz just grabs you. I don't know how to describe it to the man in the street: it's a bit like winning the pools and hearing that your baby's been born, all rolled into one. It's something that I will always remember and I'm sad that it will probably never happen again.

The first time that I was called up, I was genuinely in awe of the likes of Lineker and John Barnes, people whom I had always admired. But Lawrie McMenemy told me I shouldn't be worried about being alongside them, that I had earned the right to be there on my own, and that smoothed the way. The thing about England is that, no matter how big a superstar you are at your club, everybody's the same once they pull on a white shirt. And when you see that people like Lineker have as much time for you as you have for them, then you get a real glow of satisfaction.

I know that my England career may not have been the longest, but I also know not a second of it was wasted when I was able to work alongside Gary. He taught me so much about the runs I should make, one run for the defender and a separate one for myself, and about timing my run into the box and relaxing just before a shot or header. On England trips I used to pick his brain all the time and the stuff he taught me was of a different class, and I don't care what anybody says about him, I am in awe of the man.

The one thing that will always stay with me is that goal I scored in Poland that saved our lives. If we had not got a result out there, that would have virtually been it, we could kiss the World Cup goodbye. I was on the bench with Gary Pallister and Lee Sharpe and we were laughing and joking, but suddenly we all went deadly quiet because the Poles had started so well and had gone one up, and we realised that this could be it for all of us – curtains, the big *adios*.

Taylor called Nigel Clough over and gave him his instructions in fluent Martian and then told me to get stripped. He was trying to tell me things but I was only half listening – I was more interested in what was happening on the pitch. He was haranguing me with, 'Ian, I want you to get into holes, be busy and work around the frontal areas,' and I'm thinking, 'That's rubbish, if I was on from the start I'd have already been able to do something.' My first touch was blinding. David Bardsley drilled this ball into me, I took it on my thigh and hit a great shot, only for the referee to call me back for handball. I thought to myself, 'Yeah, that just about sums it up for me and my England career!'

Then John Barnes and Tony Dorigo played a nice couple of touches and Tony played in a perfect ball. All I can remember is being in oceans and oceans of space and thinking 'If I get a good contact, then this is going in even if the goalie gets a hand to it.'

Looking at the tape, it was an extremely difficult chance because I was coming in at pace and the ball was arriving on the half-volley at speed. If I'd missed it I would have been hung, drawn and quartered. Instead it was like the big hand coming out of the sky and a booming voice saying, 'It's you!' I could imagine all the pubs around the country and all the critics who've slaughtered me jumping for joy. And all I thought was, 'Yes, get in. Have some of that, you bastards!' It was a goal that meant something, not just a two-bob goal when we were leading 3–0. I'd got off the mark for England with a goal that got us a 1–1 draw and would have everybody talking the next day .

Trouble was, from there we went on to Norway, and got beaten 2–0. Tactically, Taylor muffed everything up. It was a shambles, a debacle and we just didn't know what we were doing, which just about sums him up as far as I'm concerned. Looking back, the saddest thing for me was that my first goal for England was buried under the weight of criticism for

Taylor when we returned home after the Norway game. I got a lot of pleasure out of playing for my country and it's tough not to be part of it still, but I've got nothing to thank Graham Taylor for; he did nothing except give me my first cap.

10
The Fire in
my Belly

Playing for a great club like Arsenal is something that I will always be proud of, but the average guy in the street just doesn't realise the problems it can also bring. That sounds crazy when we earn great wages, can afford the best cars and clothes and are treated like stars at times. But sometimes the spotlight can be so intense that it makes life difficult, not just for the player but also his family.

When I moved to Arsenal from Palace, I suddenly realised just what that spotlight meant. At Palace, nobody paid any attention to you except in south London, and then it was pretty easy to handle. Yet as soon as I signed for Arsenal, I could hardly move for photographers and reporters: they camped outside my house, all wanting a quote or a picture from me and my girlfriend, Deborah.

It was exactly the same on the pitch. I wasn't doing anything different than I was at Palace, but there was an incredible hype surrounding me because I was Arsenal's record signing. It was brilliant when I was scoring and my name was splashed all over the papers, and I'd be a liar if I said I didn't enjoy that sort of fame. But the down side to it was that if I ever stepped out of line, then the exposure would be just as great. It was only when I suddenly realised how big Arsenal were and how high profile any

Arsenal player is, that I began to get into trouble on the pitch.

I've never been a saint as far as discipline on the pitch is concerned, I would be the first to admit that. Even at school and with teams like Ten Em Bee, I was in trouble a fair bit. The only difference between those times and my professional career was that if I got suspended in the old days, I'd play the next week under a false name and just pray that nobody ever twigged!

As much as the papers build you up and give you all the adulation when you've done something good, they also go to town on you and hammer you when you've done something out of order. I can handle that and I can accept that, but even now it really depresses me when my name is blasted all over the back pages for the slightest thing. And I think I've had more than my fair share of hammerings. Because what is said in the papers is reflected in life, and suddenly I was finding that referees were giving me more attention than I was used to, that I was being pulled up for things that I had always done at Palace. They were just minor things, but suddenly doubt began to creep into my mind that referees and linesmen just weren't willing to give me the benefit of the doubt over anything. That may sound paranoid, but to me it was a frightening thing to think that people had assumed my whole character had changed just because I'd moved a few miles across London.

It didn't help that a few players who I thought were mates crawled out of the woodwork ready to stick the knife in. Step forward Ken Monkou ... It's only just recently that I've been able to speak to Ken again after what he did to me in one newspaper. We'd had a real tussle when Arsenal played Southampton. Both of us were really getting stuck in and I don't think there were too many holds barred. I didn't think too much about it afterwards, but perhaps Ken had the right hump because I'd scored and played well and Arsenal had won, because the next day he absolutely went to town on me. It was splashed across two pages how my whole game was based on intimidation and trying to hurt people. I couldn't believe that a fellow player would strike at another in cold blood like that, and that's why him and me have had a major problem until last season.

The awful thing was that a week later, everything that he said was brought up again in a far worse way because of the incident that I had with David Howells in our North London derby match against Spurs back in November 1992. There are very few things that I've regretted in my life, but that was one of them, because it just reinforced the impression that I was some out-of-control nutcase, ready to kick or punch anybody who got in my way. The whole thing with Howells must have been over in a fraction of a second, but it left a permanent scar on my reputation. North London matches are as passionate as just about any other derby in the world, tempers are at boiling point right from the word go, and it only takes the slightest thing to spark off trouble. Dave and I had a flare-up in the first half – nothing out of order, but we both felt there was that edge to it, and I think a lot of the other lads realised that if anything was going to go off it would be between us two. That feeling carried over into the second half and I suppose it was just a matter of time before it got out of hand.

The flashpoint came when he fouled me, and I just snapped. The red mist came down and before I knew what I was doing, I gave him a slap. I know it looked bad on the telly and I accept that I was stupid even to have raised my hand. I am in no way trying to make excuses for what I did, but it wasn't the sort of punch that would have laid anybody out. It was a gut reaction – a wrong one – and one that I will probably regret for the rest of my life.

Suddenly, my whole world collapsed. I couldn't believe I was the same person that all the newspapers were writing about, the mad-eyed nutter who was a danger to himself and football, or the crazy man who was so pumped up that he couldn't control his actions on the pitch. I knew that the reaction was going to be huge but I just didn't realise that for three days running I would be the most hated man in British football. The papers did absolutely everything. They put a picture of my head on a cartoon body lying on a psychiatrist's couch and got some self-styled shrink to analyse just what was supposed to be going on in my head. They took a picture of me celebrating a goal and did an analysis of my body language that said I was so pumped up during a match that there was no way I could be in control and that I was dangerous. It hit me hard that I could be the centre of all this attention and I knew then and there that I had to change.

It was David Rocastle and George Graham who got through to me. I was disappointed that I could have let myself get carried away on the pitch, but I also knew it was just a one-off that would probably never happen again. Rocky told me that nobody could criticise me for the way that I played, so they would always be looking for something else to drag me down with and that I should never give them that opportunity.

George was more to the point! He slaughtered me and told me that I was a disgrace to myself and a disgrace to Arsenal and that he wouldn't put up with another incident like the Howells affair. But he also told me that it was the fire in my belly that made me such an effective player and that I should never lose that, just learn how to control it.

I got a three-match ban but no fine from the FA, and I could handle that because I put my hands up and admitted that I was totally out of order. What I couldn't handle was the way that I was portrayed. It hurt Deborah as well because every time she walked out of the house people would be looking at her as if there was something wrong with her, that she must have a screw loose to be going out with a guy who was supposed to be crazy. It made me realise that life at Arsenal was a goldfish bowl, and anything I did on the pitch affected my life – and my family's life – off it. It also made me determined never to put Deborah through anything like that again.

The crazy thing is me and Howells finally got it sorted out last summer. Both Arsenal and Spurs were in Hong Kong on a pre-season tour and a lot of the players were drinking in the same bar. It was pretty late and we'd all had a few when one of the Spurs boys shouted across to me, 'OK, Wrighty, Dave has a free shot at you after all these years.' I just went along with it and Howells lined up to punch me smack in the face when at the last moment he dived forward, grabbed my face and gave me the biggest, wettest kiss I've ever had. That's the way it should be, and could be if we were just left alone to sort things out without cameras focused on us every second of the day.

But the Howells incident finally convinced me that the disciplinary side of things was beginning to overshadow what I was achieving through my goals. Yet however hard I tried to go 'straight' everything just kept piling up on me, and even to this day I have been unable to shake off the fact that people are just waiting for me to step over the line so they can hammer me. Arsenal have been brilliant and they've stood by me every step of the way, but I think that I have to accept that authority and I are never, ever going to see eye to eye. It's like a convicted burglar who comes out of the nick determined never to break the law again, but as soon as there's a burglary on his manor, the Old Bill drag him in without a second thought.

To my mind, that's how it is with me and referees. I'm never going to be anything but a bad boy as far as a some of them are concerned. I really do feel that the standard of refereeing from some officials has dropped over the last two or three years: there are now so many that are completely unapproachable and won't even talk to you, let alone have a laugh and a joke like some of the old guys used to. There are certain referees these days who are making massive mistakes which are costing people jobs and causing all kinds of heartache. Now that's not all their fault because some of the rules they have to enforce are ridiculous, especially after the directives that came in from FIFA last season that took away all their decision-making power and limited their applying simple common sense. Before, a referee could make his own mind up as to what sort of decision he would take based on how the game was going: now he has to make a certain stand or he gets into trouble himself.

However, having said that, I would just love referees to be more human and to try and put themselves in the player's position once in a while. For many, the consistency has deteriorated, the sense of humour has gone and now they just turn up like robots, make dreadful decisions and then leave while the rest of us – players and managers – are left wondering what the hell hit us.

There are a few exceptions. Keith Cooper has hit me with a few yellow cards in his time, but I know he's a good refer-ee and I can accept his decisions. The same goes for Alan Wilkie. He's one of the few that you can actually talk to and get along with and it feels as if he's got a bit of sympathy for the players. Dermot Gallagher is all right, he's one that I get along with and I think he understands where I'm coming from. There are others who do their job, but to my mind don't do it as well as they can. I know it's a tough job and the game is so fast nowadays that sometimes it's hard to keep pace with, but if they can't take the heat then they have to get out of the kitchen. I'll tell you something: if I had as many bad games for Arsenal as some referees have every season, then you'd never see me – I'd be stuck in the reserves. But nothing seems to happen to referees. They make a howler of a decision which is quite obvious to everybody, but do they get dropped for a couple of games? Do they, hell! They're back the next week in charge of a huge match as if nothing has happened.

One referee I have a big problem with is Robbie Hart. Arsenal played Norwich a couple of seasons back and in my opinion he made some dreadful decisions, and afterwards to the press I called him a 'muppet'. It wasn't meant as anything derogatory, it was just that he might as well have been a puppet because every move he made seemed to be with the aim of impressing the people above him, and carried out without an ounce of common sense. I got into trouble because of that, and Arsenal made me send a letter of apology to him. I wish I'd saved the paper, because since that day, almost every time he's refereed one of our matches, he's booked me!

Last season was so frustrating because I got booked for diving, something that I have never, ever done in my whole career. Anybody who knows me will tell you that I'm a lot of things, but I've never been a diver because it's one of the things that I hate most in football. Incredibly, it was Jeff Winter who did me. He's a man whom I've got a lot of time for because he can be one of the lads who likes a bit of a joke and laugh, and generally lets the players get on with things. But he was seventy yards away when Gareth Southgate tackled me at Villa, and even though Gareth stood up and said he had fouled me, Winter refused to overturn his decision. Gareth was willing to go to the FA and say that I'd been caught; instead, Winter refused to back down and that was it: more disciplinary points and another suspension just to add to my problems.

That really hurt me because it was in effect a case of the referee calling me a cheat. That's what it boils down to at the end of the day and that's what really kicks me in the guts. The incident was a couple of minutes from the end of the game. I was chasing a through ball and if I'd got it, then I would have had a chance to score. Knowing my game and my character, does Winter honestly believe I'd give that up just for the sake of a dive and a free kick? I have never cheated to try and score a goal because I've got more about me than that, so why the hell would I do it when I had a golden opportunity? I would never want to give anybody the chance to call me a cheat, but that's effectively what Winter's done with that one decision.

I just wish the referees could be more human. I would love to take somebody like David Elleray out for a meal and a drink and just sit down and talk to him for a couple of hours to try and get the players' point of view over to him in the hope that it would open his eyes. David and I don't see eye to eye at the best of times. He's a schoolmaster and treats players as if they're back in the playground or they've forgotten their homework instead of adults playing a tough game for big rewards. I'd just like to see him relax a bit, let the players talk to him and make himself more approachable. At the moment he's so uptight, you can't even talk to the guy without worrying that he's going to fish in his pocket for a yellow card. I sometimes think he'd be happier dishing out detention or lines in school.

David booked me once at Leicester, which I couldn't believe. Paul Dickov and I were getting kicked from one end of Filbert Street to the other and we had not been given a thing all first half. I started to ask him for some protection, but all he said was, 'Go away, I don't want to talk to you.' So at half-time we were heading down the tunnel and I turned to him to say something and he booked me straight away before I'd virtually opened my mouth. What the hell chance do you stand when someone acts like that? I didn't even get a chance to put my opinion over without him waving a card in my face.

There have been times in my career when I've just wanted to go up to a referee and beg him for some protection because I'm sure they were all defenders in a past life. There are defenders walking about in the Premiership who must have a special pair of boots just reserved for kicking me. They bring them out twice a season, polish them, give them a kiss before they go to bed and promise them that they'll be let loose on Wrighty the next day. But if you try and point that out to a referee, it's 'I make the decisions, just go away', so you shrug your shoulders, take the battering and count the bruises in the bath afterwards.

Bruce Rioch has told me not to talk to referees any more, but it's virtually impossible. Even when I keep my mouth shut some referees will come up to me and say, 'What's the matter, Wrighty, have you got the hump or something?' So how the hell can I win? Away games are the worst for me because most of the trouble that comes from referees happens because the crowd provoke it. I just wish I could go up to a referee before the game and say, 'Look, if I do something bad, then I don't mind getting hammered. But just because the crowd goes mental don't automatically think I'm to blame because it's not always the case.' I have had to say that to some officials, and perhaps they've taken it on board: I'd like to think so.

I'd like the Football Association to send some kind of observer to a couple of away games and just listen to the abuse the opposition striker gets. It's not just me, but virtually every other forward in the country will tell you the same thing. When they go away, they get dog's abuse from the first minute to the last. If that's happening every time they go for a challenge, then in the end it's bound to sway a referee at least once in a match. Of course, sometimes I deserve to get pulled up but it seems to me that I am getting far more than my fair share of criticism from referees.

My run-ins with referees usually end up with me in hot water with the FA. I know I'm supposed to be careful about what I say or I'm going to get slapped down again, but this is the one chance I've got to say what I think and I can't pass up the opportunity to tell it how I see it.

In the 1993/94 season I was the first player to reach 41 disciplinary points. Only two of those bookings were for dissent, and one of those came down to kicking the ball away, so it's obvious that the majority of the yellow cards were for tackles. Now any player in the country will tell you that I am not a dirty player. Most of my bookings are for over-enthusiasm when I'm trying to stop a defender getting away. That didn't exactly cut it with the FA and they slammed me with a four-game ban and a record £1,000 fine. Within a few weeks however, United's Steve Bruce was up before them. What did he get? A two-game ban and a £250 fine.

Now you tell me, where is the justice in that?

There have been so many other occasions where I've felt as if I'm being singled out that I've almost lost count. I got fined five grand for swearing and making an obscene gesture at a linesman during the FA Cup Final replay against Sheffield Wednesday three years ago. The TV cameras captured it and the FA thought that was such an outrage that I was charged with bringing the game into disrepute. I was actually on honeymoon at the time when the news came over the radio, which, I have to say, didn't exactly please me or Deborah. The sickening thing was that the FA thought me calling a linesman a f*****g w****r was far worse than when Mark Bright splattered Andy Linighan's nose all across his face with a blatant elbow. Now Brighty is my best mate and I would never criticise him, but is swearing a worse crime than battering a fellow player? I know what I think. When the Sky analyser Andy Gray ran through it on TV, it showed that Mark really didn't have any intention of going for the ball and in his heart he knows that's true. To me, that's far more damaging to football than me swearing. The FA said they had received numerous letters of protest after what I did. Well, all I can say is that those people have got the saddest of sad lives.

The season after I got fined for making the w****r sign to a linesman, Vinny Samways did exactly the same thing to Terry Phelan when Spurs were playing Manchester City in a live televised game. It was right there on millions of television sets throughout the country, but was there any action taken against Vinny? Was there, hell! The lads all came into training the next day and asked me if I'd seen it. Of course I had, but what could I say?

The worst thing about all this is that my brushes with authority represent the only negative aspects in my life at the moment. Things couldn't be better for me, because I've got a wonderful wife and family, I'm still playing well for one of the greatest clubs in the world and things are sweet. Yet just when I think, 'Yeah, man, I'm cruising here,' I seem to run head-first into authority, and my world comes crashing down again.

Bruce Rioch has made it perfectly plain that he won't put up with any disciplinary problems, but even he could see last season just what I'm up against sometimes. He appealed to Jeff Winter, whom he knows pretty well, to have another look at the 'diving' decision, because Bruce could see the injustice in it. He was just as disappointed as I was when there was no change and I was given the disciplinary points. I don't want to miss matches through suspension, and the boss doesn't want his top scorer in the stand when I should be out there winning games for Arsenal. I missed ten games in 1994-95 through suspension and I don't want that to happen ever again.

I was determined to start last season by just playing my natural game, to steer clear of any trouble and show the new manager just what I was capable of. But it started almost immediately in some of the pre-season friendly games. I went to Sweden and got booked a couple of times for tackles that were so tame that my two-year-old son Stacey could have ridden them. Then I had a run-in with some player at

Southend who seemed to want a piece of me to take home and put on his mantelpiece. He was kicking lumps out of me every time I went near the ball, but the moment there was a 50-50 challenge which I went for just as hard as he did, I got booked! The mad thing was that that booking counted in the totting-up of my points, and that's why I was banned for three games before we'd even got to Christmas.

It was then that Bruce Rioch realised that perhaps there was a different agenda for me at times and although it might be tough for him to take, I think he accepts that I am going to get booked more than any other Arsenal player. The thing is that no matter how many times I get booked, banned or fined, I will not change my natural game. If I was ever to leave Arsenal, I know there would be a queue of clubs after me because of the enthusiasm of my game, my desire to win and my willingness to go all out for it. That's what has made me successful over the years, that's what has made me the club's top scorer and that's what the fans like about my game. If I suddenly switched styles just to avoid getting into trouble, what do you think would happen? I'll tell you: the goals would dry up because I wouldn't be busting a gut to get into the vital positions, my team-mates would be on my back and the fans would slaughter me, because I know how their minds work. If I let a defender out just because to tackle him might get me a booking, I'd be lampooned by every single Arsenal fan in the ground.

I should know better, I suppose, because I missed Arsenal's first European Cup Winners' Cup Final through suspension, and it robbed me of one of the greatest days of my life. But the bottom line is that I would rather sit out half the season through suspension than lose the fire in my belly and become half the player I am today.

Thankfully, I've always had that something inside me that pulls me back from going right over the edge. There have been times when I've just wanted to chin a referee, but that little voice tells me that my football career would be finished and that's enough to pull me up short of taking that next step. Even when I was younger and playing park football I've always had just enough restraint to keep a lid on it … and I thank God for that because there have been times when I've only been an inch away from losing it in a big, big way.

11
Cup Dreams

I won the three greatest prizes of my life in 1993: an FA Cup winners' medal, a League Cup winners' medal and a beautiful wife. Deborah and I decided that it was about time we did the right thing and got married, and the wedding in Mauritius capped my most successful ever season in football as far as honours were concerned. It was an incredible year, one in which Arsenal went to Wembley four times in as many months and walked away with a cup double that no other club had ever achieved.

But nothing could ever match the pride I felt on my wedding day. The only problem with the wedding was that neither of our families were in Mauritius to see it. It goes without saying that nothing in my life could run ever smoothly and, even though Deb would have loved a major white wedding in England, there were so many family problems that it made it impossible. My mum is a wonderful woman, but she can be really difficult to get along with, and she and my mother-in-law-to-be had a massive fall-out about a year before we were due to get married. The atmosphere between the two families was really bad, so in the end Deb and I just thought we would go ahead anyway. It was our day, and we didn't want anything or anybody to spoil it, so we disappeared off to the island of Mauritius and got married on the beach with just Mark Bright and Mitchell Thomas there as guests. In the end it was a perfect day, and the only thing that spoiled the honeymoon was the news from England that I'd been fined five-grand for swearing at a linesman during the FA Cup Final replay!

It wasn't exactly a whirlwind romance with Deborah. We go back a long way; having grown up together on the same estate and gone to the same parties, and after we met up again years later, it was virtually love at second sight – at least for me. My proposal wasn't exactly romantic, I have to admit. We were driving home from a local Italian restaurant when I just turned to Deb and said, 'Do you fancy getting married? And if so, can you handle being my wife for the next fifty years?' I think she was just as surprised as I was that I'd popped the question, but it didn't take her too long to accept.

As I said, our wedding was just about the perfect way to round off a season that went beyond anything that I'd ever dreamed about. The pinnacle of my career so far had been to play in a Wembley final and I never thought I would experience the same thrill as when I went there with Palace. But to walk away from that ground and to look back at the Twin Towers knowing that you've got a winners' medal in your pocket is a feeling I can never really describe. To do it twice within three months is out of this world.

That season shut a lot of people up as far as Arsenal were concerned. The year before had been a complete nightmare in the cup competitions because we went out to Wrexham in the third round of the FA Cup and then got absolutely slaughtered by Benfica in the European Champions Cup. I hadn't played in either of those games because I'd joined Arsenal too late to qualify to play in Europe and I was suspended for the Wrexham match. But sitting there watching the lads and knowing there was nothing I could do about it, was a really painful experience. The Benfica defeat I could accept to a degree because that was one of the greatest displays I've ever seen from a club side: they simply overwhelmed us at Highbury and taught us a lesson that would stand us in good stead in the next few seasons.

But the Wrexham game was different. Jimmy Carter had a perfectly good goal disallowed, and suddenly I knew that everything was stacked against us and we would be lucky to come away with even a draw. Then Welshman Mickey Thomas pulled off the sort of goal that was a once in a life-time, a free kick that if he took it another thousand times would never steam into the top corner as it did that after-noon. Wrexham's second was even worse, a shot that drib-bled over the line with just enough pace and angle to beat David Seaman, but that everybody thought he could have stopped.

I was sitting in the directors' box and nearly belted this Welsh bloke who was giving David Rocastle some horrible racial abuse. On hearing him shout 'black bastard' when Rocky got the ball, I was out of my seat before anybody could stop me. We were face-to-face, and he was panicking and kept insisting he'd only said '*that* bastard'. Considering the state I was in, I would have smacked him one if one of the other lads hadn't pulled me back into my seat and warned the idiot to keep his mouth shut. The mood in the Arsenal dressing room after that game was desperate.

The team got a lot of criticism for those couple of results and George Graham took stock and decided that from now on he was going to produce an Arsenal side that would pick up a cup the next season. He knew, and the players all knew, that we just weren't consistent enough to win the champion-ship. George wanted to strengthen the squad, but there weren't the players around at the time to achieve that, so he stuck with the lads he had and made us into the sort of unit that would in the following seasons scare the living daylights out of other sides in the cup competitions. We were saying at

Highbury that in a one-off game we could beat anybody in the country. It didn't matter if it was Liverpool or Wrexham, we knew we could win without a shadow of a doubt. And if we didn't get knocked out in the first round, we fancied ourselves to go on and win the tournament.

We also had to make amends for the season before, and George and all the players felt that little buzz which told us that this was going to be our year. I knew I had to get on and win something because all I had to show for my efforts was a ZDS trophy medal which, to my mind, doesn't count. I'd never give it up, but when I came to Arsenal and heard Paul Merson and Tony Adams reel off all the trophies that the club had won, I kept my head down and tried not to mention Palace's ZDS trophy, otherwise I'd be slaughtered.

I think we all caught the mood when we had to play Yeovil away in the third round of the FA Cup. By that time we were on a bit of a roll in the League Cup because we'd beaten the dreaded Millwall, thanks to some brilliant goalkeeping from David Seaman in a penalty shoot-out and then got through 3–2 on aggregate against Derby.

But it was against Yeovil that suddenly we knew deep down that we were unbeatable. It was the sort of game that everybody was expecting us to make a mess of, especially after Wrexham, and I will never forget the sight of all the photographers and reporters at that game just licking their lips and waiting for us to fail. George even made it part of his team talk: he told us that the whole country wanted us to fail and we should send the press home with their tails between their legs. But it didn't matter how much George tried to build it up, I was still frightened of Yeovil because they had that old Cup tradition and were a quite a useful non-league side.

I needn't have lost too much sleep because in the event we steamrollered them. For ten minutes we kept them quiet and from then on it was one-way traffic. If you don't let small teams like that score in the first twenty minutes, you should really be safe because then you can grind them down, start to play and score goals. We won 3–1 and I scored a hat-trick, but again people were trying to bring me down with lies.

I was getting bad abuse from the Yeovil fans, so when I scored my hat-trick I put three fingers up behind my head just to rub it in for them, but some cunning photographer took the shot so it looked like I was giving them the V-sign. So that story was splashed all over the back pages and took all the headlines away from my hat-trick and Arsenal's good win. I'll tell you, I was as devastated as I've ever been in my life, because I knew I hadn't done anything, but it still looked as if that one action had taken all the praise away from the lads. Some fool reporters went for the 'Why does he have to spoil it?' rubbish, and I even considered taking legal action, but at the end of the day it would have just given the idiots more mileage when all I wanted was for people to forget it. Look in the record books today and all it says is that I scored a hat-trick, not that I got criticised because of a picture from some snidey photographer.

Those three goals put me on an FA Cup roll. I scored in every round except the semi-final and I just couldn't wait for those games to come around because I just had this gut, instinctive feeling that I was going to get a goal. All the boys were right behind me because they could see I was on fire and there was the buzz going round the club that this was *our* year, make no mistake.

There's always one cup game in a season that you dread, and for me it was in the League Cup and it was Scarborough away. It seems that Arsenal always get lumbered with those sort of games. I've lost count of the times we've had to go up to some ramshackle northern ground in the wind, the rain or the snow, and grind out a 1–0 win, thank God for the final whistle and then get on the coach and get the hell away from there. Scarborough was exactly like that. It was freezing and foggy and I didn't think that the game was going to be played because you could hardly see one side of the pitch from the other, but we just got on with the job, beat them 1–0 and said *adios* to sunny Scarborough!

From then on the Cup games seemed to become a blur. It was as if we were playing one virtually every week and, to be fair, we forgot all about the league. George wasn't exactly pleased that our league form wasn't much to shout about but I think he was just as caught up in our Cup run as the players and supporters were.

We beat Leeds in the fourth round of the FA Cup after drawing 2–2 at our place. The replay was incredible, the atmosphere at Elland Road was like nothing I'd ever experienced at a league ground, even in a north London derby. White Hart Lane may have an intimi-dating atmosphere but I'll tell you something, that night in Leeds sent shivers down my spine because their fans really hated us for ninety minutes. We won 3–2, and I scored twice, and suddenly I had this feeling that our name was on the Cup. We'd come through a match in a hostile atmosphere at one of the toughest grounds in the country on which to get a result, and suddenly we were walking nine feet tall.

The Cup has this habit of throwing the same teams together all the time, so it seems as if you're playing them every week. It was like that with Nottingham Forest that year. We got drawn against them in the fifth round of both cups, and then in between we played them in the league, and in the end we knew them so well that it was ridiculous. But we also knew that they couldn't hurt us and although they were hard games, we beat them 2–0 twice to get into the semi-final of the League Cup and the last eight of the FA Cup.

The League Cup semi-final involved a two-legged game with Crystal Palace, something that I was looking forward to with mixed feelings. I thought I had left the club on good terms; I'd never said a word about the players, the fans or anything and I would have loved to have got on with every-body connected with Palace. But earlier in the season when we'd played them at Highbury, I got such a roasting from the Palace supporters that it almost broke my heart.

These were people who I had virtually grown up with, people who had cheered me when things had gone well and lifted me in the bad days at places like Anfield when we'd been hammered. I would have liked to have given them something back. Instead, I turned completely against them after the way they reacted at Highbury, as I explained earlier, and I was so pleased to have scored a goal which went some way to shutting the morons up.

Before the semi-final I also got hate mail sent to my home and to Highbury and it wasn't just the usual rubbish – it was racist and nasty and it really shook me that people with whom I'd been connected just eighteen months before now wanted to hurt me so badly.

The first leg was at Selhurst Park and we just crushed them. It was 3–1 at the end, but it could have been five or six, and I've never been so delighted to have scored. The home leg at Highbury was a formality which we won 2–0 and I scored again, although this time I was just satisfied to have done my job.

So that was it, we were at Wembley and were still bang on course for another final after we beat Ipswich 4–2 in the quarter-finals. But before we even started to look at the FA Cup Final, there was the biggest game that Arsenal had played in two years – Spurs in the semi-final and it was obvi-ous that match *had* to be played at Wembley.

I've got a vivid imagination, but even I wouldn't have dreamt up another north London semi-final at Wembley. To think that only two years after Spurs had handed Arsenal the biggest humiliation in their history when they beat us 3–1, we had a chance to go out and get revenge … that was just something that seemed beyond belief. I'd been at that game and I'd seen what it did to a few of my Arsenal mates but, being at Palace at the time, I couldn't understand how badly it could hurt to lose to Spurs.

I've got to put a few things in perspective here. I don't hate Spurs, in fact I'm good mates with players like Ian Walker and Teddy Sheringham whom I've known from his days at Millwall. I even quite like Spurs fans. They come up to me when I'm out and say how they wish I was playing for them instead of Arsenal, and we can have a drink and a bit of a laugh. But when there is a derby coming up, the whole build-up goes onto another planet and that to me is what football is all about. The pressure and the expectancy is so high that you can't escape it for a minute: wherever you go there's somebody saying, 'Stuff Spurs for us Wrighty,' or 'You're gonna get mashed on Saturday.' And in recent years it's even gone beyond the bounds of just fanaticism – there's now a nasty edge to it. The season before last at Highbury, a Spurs fan threw an empty whisky bottle at me which would have done me major damage if the fella hadn't been such a poor shot.

So you can imagine what the build-up to the semi-final was like – a thousand times more intense! The Arsenal fans had had to put up with 'We beat the scum 3–1' for two years without ever being able to hit back. And there were still some pretty raw scars in our dressing room after that match. People like 'Merse' and Tony Adams, who are Arsenal to the core, took that defeat pretty badly and had been waiting for this opportunity to put the record straight and wipe out the humiliation of two years before.

There was so much talk in the press about this game that for us it seemed like the final itself. You could almost forget that Sheffield Wednesday were playing Sheffield United the day before and that there was the possibility of a double Arsenal versus Wednesday final on the cards. All the talk was us against Spurs, nothing else mattered.

There was so much pressure surrounding the game that it even got through to George. Normally he's the calmest man around: nothing flaps him, he takes it all in his stride, lets it wash over him and just gets on with the business. But this time the nerves had got to him and when he's nervous, his brain goes. We were staying at the Sopwell House Hotel near to our training ground at St Albans and George was going through the Spurs side, writing their names on a board, and I swear, he must have spelt every name in their team wrong! He was scribbling things out, getting them wrong again and the boys were laughing their heads off.

But we didn't need a team talk. This was the chance we – and all the fans – had been waiting for to exorcise the ghost of that last game at Wembley where Gazza and Lineker had put the boot in.

The actual game was rubbish, just like all the other derbies. It was just on a bigger scale, and at Wembley. But I didn't care because I knew that God, or whoever, was smiling on us from the moment that Andy Linighan brought down Darren Anderton and the referee didn't give a penalty. The more I look at it, the more it's obvious to me that it was a penalty because Andy *did* catch Darren and the Spurs man went down. Sometimes I wonder what goes through a referee's mind, because he only has to look at an incident and see who is involved if he has any doubt, and Darren is not the sort of player to dive or make a meal of things, so that should have told the referee something. But I'm not going to start slagging the referee off because that one decision swung the game in our favour, no doubt about it. There weren't too many chances in the game, although I had a shot that I thought was going in until Erik Thorstvedt stuck up a hand to push it away, and at the other end, Vinny Samways had one excellent chance that he should have done better with.

But if anybody was going to win the game, then I couldn't pick a better man to do it than Tony Adams. What a player!

Tony's just the sort of professional that I take my hat off to in football. It all happened in slow motion, just like the most vital goals always seem to. It was typical Arsenal, a set-piece, Tony getting away from everybody at the back post and getting above the Spurs defence to head the ball past Erik – just incredible. The win and the goal meant so much to Tony, and that's why at the end of the match he just crouched down and was overcome with emotion as all the fans were singing, 'Donkey won the derby', the players jumping over each other and crying and laughing all at the same time.

I feel for anybody who loses in a semi-final. Take it from me, losing a final has to be easier to accept because at least you've got there and you can say you took part on the big day and your name will go down in the history books, but losing in a semi-final seems like all that hard work and slog that you've put in means nothing. There's no glory attached to losing a semi-final: you're a nobody, and that is hard to handle because you cannot put it out of your mind and forget it. Looking at the Spurs players and Terry Venables at the end, even a bit of my heart went out to them.

As soon as we got through, Sheffield Wednesday must have been thinking it was time to pack up and go home. We'd already beaten them in the Coca-Cola Cup and they were the sort of side that even if we played badly against them, we'd still win. Even if we turned up with just eight men, there was no way they could have beaten us. When the draw for the FA Cup was made last season and it came up, 'Arsenal will play Sheffield...' everybody at Hillsborough must have been wetting themselves. Instead, we got United. Not that it made much difference to Wednesday, they went out to Charlton. Mind you, we didn't exactly cover ourselves in glory...

The fact that we were playing Wednesday twice at Wembley did strange things to me and Brighty, who had left Palace to join Wednesday in 1992. Ever since he came to

Palace, all we've ever talked about was winning medals and cups and playing at Wembley. Like me, he's solely motivated by success and winning things, that is what gives us that edge. Now we were going to be head-to-head twice in the same season and one of us was going to be the loser. I said at the end of that season that I just wished Wednesday had won the League Cup and we'd gone on to win the FA Cup so that Brighty could have got a taste of what it felt like to be the victor once. Looking back, that's a stupid thing to have said because really you have to want to win every single game, but I can honestly say there was something inside me that would have traded my winners' medal for one of his losers'.

Obviously the press all wanted to do a piece with us about what it would be like for two best mates to come up against each other at a showpiece event, but we tried to play all the hype down. In fact, our relationship was going through a difficult patch. There wasn't exactly anything strained between us, but it felt awkward talking on the phone because we didn't want to let our true feelings out, and in the end we gave up even talking for about a fortnight before that first final.

When we won the League Cup I didn't feel so bad because I knew it was the FA Cup that Brighty wanted more than anything. So when we won that as well, and people blamed him for letting Andy Linighan score the winner in the replay, I was churned up inside. I couldn't contain my happiness, but I also cried for my best mate because that was the third time he'd been in a big final and come away with nothing. I drank some champagne in the dressing room afterwards, got a bit drunk and then suddenly wondered what Brighty was doing. I know there was nothing in the whole world that I could say or do to make the guy feel good.

But although I felt bad for Brighty, I was absolutely delighted to have given Wednesday a beating – twice! John Harkes did something really stupid before the first game, he went on record as saying Arsenal were nothing but Wimbledon with 'A-levels', not exactly something that was going to endear him to us. Just before we came down the tunnel, I shouted down his ear, 'You w*****, we'll show you who's Wimbledon with A-levels!' Carlton Palmer was just behind him and told him not to worry about it, but I could tell that Carlton was very worried that we were so fired up for it.

Again the match was not the best, and nobody ever remembers the game, just the aftermath and the tragedy of Steve Morrow. He had just won the Cup for us, had played out of his skin in midfield and what happened to him afterwards was a tragedy-and-a-half and it's something that no Arsenal player who was there will ever forget. It seemed like a harmless joke when Tony Adams flipped him over his shoulder and even when he didn't get up straight away, nobody took too much notice. Suddenly it dawned on us all that this was serious and that Stevie was in a bad way. When we saw the state of his arm and the angle at which it was hanging from his shoulder, it almost made me want to be sick. I've never seen an injury that horrible in all my time in football.

Stevie was rushed off to hospital, and all of a sudden there didn't seem too much reason to celebrate. Tony was gutted; in tears and obviously distraught, and none of us were able to console him. It was a one-off thing that was meant to be a joke but it turned out to be the worst thing that could have happened and unfortunately it really took the shine off the win.

In a strange way, that incident also helped us to be even more pumped up for the FA Cup Final, and Wednesday can thank their own fans for that. Some idiot came out with a banner saying, 'Was Morrow left out, or was he dropped?' Now the fans might have thought that was a laugh, but to the lads who had saw how much pain Stevie was in and the complications of the injury, it was a sickener. It really annoyed us that somebody could be that thoughtless and it stirred us up to really go for it.

In fact, Wednesday did a brilliant job of shooting themselves in the foot in the preparation for the second final. Trevor Francis came out with the theory that we'd only won because we'd stopped their flair players in the first match. Now pardon me because I may have been missing a few things over the years, but isn't that the whole point? Should we have just sat back and let Chris Waddle and John Sheridan make forty yard passes all day, or let Brighty have all the chances that his heart desired? Rubbish! We had a game plan and stuck to it brilliantly, and George wasn't going to change a thing second time around. He just took one look at what Francis had said and told us to ignore it, to go out and do it again and create a little bit of history by becoming the first side to have won both cups in the same season.

The League Cup medal was my first major medal, but it was a pitiful little thing – I had five-a-side medals from when I was a kid that were bigger! It's up in my collection but it's not exactly in pride of place. When I saw it, I just thought to myself that I had to go on and get an FA Cup winners' medal just to put that one in the shade. For me, the FA Cup final was just like the best recurring dream you could ever have. If I ever have to go through an experience like in the film *Groundhog Day*, I want it to be the day of the FA Cup final because I could go through it again, second by second, every day of my life. This time around I was able to take in so much more than when we went to Wembley with Palace; everything was so much calmer and relaxed, more professional.

The Palace boys – and I was as bad as anybody – got caught up in the occasion far too much and the match seemed to take a back seat at times. It was like a dream come true for us, and everybody loved the attention from the media and the public. You could see people getting greedy and we were more interested in making as much money out of the occasion as possible: What sponsorship deal could we do? How much were the papers going to pay us? Was the money from this interview or that interview going into the players' pool? In the end, the game hit us and we weren't as prepared as we should have been, and I think that cost us. We were the fairy-tale team and we were going to live that fairy-tale for as long as we could.

At Arsenal it was bang on the level, because this was a club that knew how to handle this sort of thing. George wouldn't let anybody in who would turn our heads and it was so in control, there wasn't anything to upset us or distract us. The only thing I was upset about was that George wouldn't let us have club suits for the final. To me, new suits are part of the FA Cup final. I used to love watching it on the telly when I was a kid, seeing all the players coming out with their matching new suits and carnations, looking the business on the pitch before the kick-off. But not George, oh no. It was club blazers and trousers and that was it, end of argument. The biggest day in the club's history for ten years and we're all wearing our crumpled club blazers that we've had for a year. He wouldn't even get us new club blazers, the Scottish skinflint! It was just 'Get on with it, Wrighty.' It might sound trivial, but to me that was all part of the occasion.

I was sweating on the day of the final because I'd broken my little toe in a tackle with Nigel Clough a week before. (I know, Nigel Clough of all people!) But I tell you, that boy tackles as hard as anybody I've ever known. I remember Gazza telling me that 'Cloughie' had almost knocked him out with a tackle once. He did one of his turns and Cloughie went straight through him, and Gazza said the whole left side of his body went numb! Now I knew exactly how he felt. Nigel was playing at the back for Forest and he went

Above: An 'encounter' against the south London boys. Robbie Earle and his Wimbledon teammates don't seem too impressed with me, but the ref isn't exactly rushing to my rescue!

Right: Sometimes I can't stop myself as far as referees are concerned, I just have to tell them where they're going wrong.

The two real loves of my life, Debbie and Stacey.

Getting a helping hand as I perfect my slam dunk. Not bad for a novice, eh?

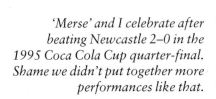

'Merse' and I celebrate after beating Newcastle 2–0 in the 1995 Coca Cola Cup quarter-final. Shame we didn't put together more performances like that.

Mud brothers. Crazy man Gazza gets me involved in some dirty business during England training.

The closest person to me in football. My biggest wish is that Incey and I could team up together before I retire from the game.

I call him the Colossus. Arsenal captain Tony Adams is the most inspirational player I have ever come across.

Above: Ton up! My 100th goal for Arsenal, at Highbury in October 1994, and I pick the perfect team to score it against – Crystal Palace. But my old team had the last laugh, winning 2–1.

Below: I've perfected a 'dying swan' routine, as Colin Hendry can testify after this foul in the Premiership match at home against Blackburn in September 1992.

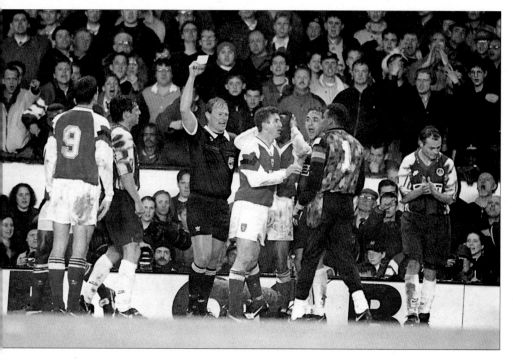

Above: Tragedy strikes as I realise this booking against Paris St Germain in the 1994 European Cup Winners' Cup semi-final second leg will keep me out of the final.

Below: Red Army. The fans welcome us home after we beat Parma in the European Cup Winners' Cup Final in Copenhagen. Although disappointed at not playing because of suspension, I was thrilled for the players and the supporters.

Above: Arsenal 1 Auxerre 0, 16 March 1995, and the goal that God blessed. My strike against the French side that got us through a tricky quarter-final tie in yet another demanding European campaign for the Gunners.

Below left and right: Joy and pain. Dave Seaman puts us into the final with his penalty saves against Sampdoria … and then Tony Adams consoles me after we lose to Zaragoza in Paris to an extra-time 'special' from former Spurs star, Nayim.

Left: Arsenal and proud. Captain for the day and I score a blinder against Everton in January 1996.

Right: OK, so he left under a cloud of suspicion but without George Graham my trophy cupboard would be a pretty bare place.

Below: Arsenal team-mate Dennis Bergkamp in full flow, and proving that the Premier League can attract the star names from abroad.

Above: Nice to be wanted. The fans make their feelings known after my transfer request of last season.

Left: No hard feelings, gaffer. Bruce Rioch and I have had our ups and downs.

Right: Could that camera be any closer? In the spotlight again for the wrong reasons as I leave Lancaster Gate following an FA disciplinary hearing to do with my comments about referees. I'm speechless.

through me like a dose of salts, all fair and square, but it felt like I'd been hit by a truck and he just caught my toe as he crunched me. I didn't know the toe was even broken, but when I came off I was sweating. I'd had injections in it for the last game of the season and that seemed to work, so I knew that I could get through the final but I wasn't 100 per cent, that's for sure.

The good thing about the toe was that I was able to make a magnificent entrance at Wembley. All the other lads were warming up and out on the pitch but I had to stay behind in the dressing rooms to have three pain-killing injections, so I was last out of the tunnel. The Wednesday fans were at the tunnel end and booed me non-stop as soon as I walked out, but when the Arsenal supporters realised what was happening they cheered me from the goalline all the way to the halfway line. What a buzz!

But if that was the reception, the noise that went up when I scored was beyond belief. Poor old Brighty fouled Lee Dixon and gave away a free kick outside the Wednesday box. Paul Davis chipped the ball onto Andy Linighan's head and as he flicked it on, I got in front and headed the ball back across Chris Woods. Then it was the old familiar Wrighty, head back, eyes closed just screaming and – surprise, surprise – I nearly burst into tears. I had to get hold of myself and say to myself, 'What the hell are you doing? There's only twenty minutes gone, for God's sake'. I learnt from the Palace final that I wasn't going to use all my energy and wear myself out like last time, so I just ran to the corner and fell on the floor and the other boys just smothered me.

In a way it was more of a thrill to score for Palace because of the double broken leg and people were saying I was lucky even to be on the bench. With Arsenal, I was in a rich vein of form and all the boys were having bets on me to score the first goal, so more was expected. But that doesn't lessen the excitement. If you want a perfect example of what it means, get a video of when Arsenal last won the Cup and take a look at Alan Sunderland's face after he scored the winner against Manchester United. That says more than I could ever put down in words.

David Hirst had to spoil my party. For once he put all his bad luck with injuries behind him and he popped up to level things up on the day, and I suppose I was pleased for him, but at the time I was appalled because I knew it was going to be a replay all over again, just like Palace against Manchester United.

In that replay, I didn't start the game and we didn't do ourselves justice. This time I knew I had to grab the opportunity with both hands because it wasn't going to be a game of untold chances, and that meant that anything that came my way I had to take. So in the second game, when Alan Smith put me through with a delightful touch inside Paul Warhurst, I knew I had to make it count. Albert – as he was known at Wednesday – was no slouch and I had to get in front of him so my first move was across his path so that he would have to foul me to stop me. All I was waiting for was for Chris Woods to make his move. I felt I'd knocked it too far and he had a chance to smother it, but he came, stopped and then came again so I just had enough time to chip it across him and into the bottom corner.

That was it. God may as well have come and taken me at that moment because it wasn't going to get much better. All I could think was that the bookies had taken a pasting because so many people had me down to score the first goal and I was pleased because my brother Morris won a few quid on me. I just thought, 'Brilliant, I've done it again,' and I knew I was in a Cup final.

The game went exactly to form and I just had a feeling that Wednesday would get something back. When Lee Dixon deflected Chris Waddle's shot past David Seaman, I knew it was going to be a slog. I couldn't last extra time because the injections had worn off and my toe was hurting so much I couldn't even run, but sitting on the bench gives you that extra dimension and distance so you can appreciate the winning goal even more.

And this one was something else. Andy Linighan had come in for Steve Bould who was injured, and the boy played like a star in that Cup run. He was brilliant in our box and in theirs, and it was fitting that somebody who'd had his nose splattered all over his face should come up with the winner in the last minute of extra time. It was like playing a game in your back garden or the school playground when you're running a John Motson style commentary: 'And it's the last minute of the game, Linighan comes up from the back, the ball's chipped in and Linighan's there, it's a goooooaaal!!!'

But amid all the joy of finally going up to collect a winner's medal at last, what I remember most is the sight of Chris Waddle crying, totally out of control and overcome with emotion. That hit me hard and I found it difficult to deal with. I couldn't trust myself to go up to him and even say anything that would make it any better. It hurt to see Chris like that because he's had as much influence on my career as anybody.

When I was at Palace and he was on fire for Spurs, we sat and talked for around two hours at the PFA dinner one year and he gave me an endless stream of good advice. He told me I could go a long way in the game if I really got my head down; he told me I had to practise finishing all the time, that I had to brush up on parts of my game that were weak, and to a kid in the old Second Division that meant a hell of a lot. That's when it dawned on me that I could make it to the top if I calmed down and worked at scoring goals. He told me the difference between the best and the also-rans was the ability to finish when the pressure was on because you only get two chances at most in a game and if you can guarantee to take one of them, you're doing the business. It was like a light bulb going on in my head and I started staying late in training, working on my shooting from all angles, my heading, and just working hard until I was confident I could take one of those two chances.

Chris changed my attitude and my whole outlook on football and now here he was, head buried in the Wembley turf, crying his eyes out.

12
On the Mark
in Europe

One of the reasons I joined Arsenal was for European football and now we had it. In fact we should have had it twice over for winning two cups, but instead somebody else got our UEFA Cup place and we went into the European Cup Winners' Cup. To my mind, we should have got a 'Get into Europe Free' card, or something like that, so that we could have traded it in at any time and waltzed straight into European competition all over again. If you win double honours you should get double the awards, so if anybody from the FA is reading this and hasn't had a heart attack yet, why don't you think about it?

But even with one shot we showed the rest of the country that we had what it took to compete with the best of the continental sides and stuff them. We weren't the prettiest side around, but we were bloody well effective, and when the chips were down we could always conjure something up and move into an extra gear. We got criticised for not playing attractive football, but we got to two finals in successive seasons, and there aren't too many British sides who can lay that card on the table. It was a testament to the players, the manager, everybody connected with Arsenal and, perhaps more than anything, the fans. I don't think they expected us to do as well as we did, but once we lifted off, I have never seen such passion from a group of supporters as the Arsenal fans showed.

Yet for me, the European matches gave me two of the lowest points of my career. First of all I missed the first final (1994) in Copenhagen, and then when I eventually did get a shot at the big prize, I was denied by probably the greatest goal I have ever seen in my life from a Moroccan who – just to make things worse – used to play for Spurs. But, I tell you something, I take my hat off to Nayim because I wish I had the skill and the bottle to go for something like that in the last minutes of a Cup final.

But Europe also gives me a great source of pride when I look at my scoring record. Playing in Europe is exactly like playing international football, and when I became the first player to score in every round leading up to our second final, it was a lovely feeling to imagine turning round to people who had written me off when I played for England and sticking two fingers up at them. Because to score in Europe, you have to have something about you. You have to have the ability to shake off the tightest markers and stick the ball in the back of the net, and that's what I was able to do in our run the season before last.

It wasn't just a case of trying to prove people wrong, it was just showing that when the opportunities came along, I could put them in as well as perhaps anybody else in Britain. And I will say to my dying day that, if I'd had similar chances for England, then there was no way that either Graham Taylor or Terry Venables would have been able to leave me out. All you have to do is ask Alan Shearer how tough it is against European and international defences. He is the business at the moment, the absolute guv'nor as far as I'm concerned, and finishing top scorer in Euro '96 was a magnificent achievement, but look how long it took him to translate goals for his club into goals for his country. European football is nothing like the Premiership where you get maybe three or four chances a game, in fact you're lucky if you get two really good chances over two legs in Europe. So when I beat Ferenc Puskas's record the season before last, it meant as much as any of the medals I've picked up, even the Golden Boot, because I was doing it against some of Europe's best.

The European games also saw me have two of the worst rows I ever had with George Graham. As far as I'm concerned, he is partly to blame for me missing the final against Parma. If he hadn't decided to play it all tactical and rest me for games where he thought it didn't matter, just to make sure I didn't get booked, then there would have been a good chance I would have served my suspension in time to play in Copenhagen. Instead, I got a yellow card against Paris St Germain in the semi-final at Highbury and that was it, out of the final and out of the greatest match of my career. I let George know about it, and he also knew about it at half-time in the PSG game when I was so distraught I just wanted to chin him – anybody – and all he did was tell me to shut up and grow up. That was just what I wanted to hear!

The friction between us started pretty early in the competition. We beat Odense in the first round: it wasn't spectacular but we went through 3–2 on aggregate so everybody was happy, including George who had always wanted to make his mark in Europe following the way in which Arsenal had gone out to Benfica a few years earlier. That game had really hurt him because people started questioning his tactical ability against European sides, and whether he had what it took to compete against the best of the continentals.

We were then drawn against Standard Liege from Belgium, and suddenly everybody started saying that this was it, the Belgians would walk all over us because they were so technically superior, they had bags of experience in Europe and it would be a case of them holding us at Highbury and then hammering us over there. That just shows what excellent judges of football some of the journalists are – I don't think that – because we absolutely murdered Liege at home 3–0 and played just about as well as any Arsenal side I have ever known.

The only problem was that George had got it into his mind that we had to show referees just what gentlemen we were on the pitch, and that if we fouled somebody then we should pick them up straight away and we wouldn't get booked. Sounds brilliant, but it was the worst piece of advice anybody has ever given me. I brought down this guy who then proceeded to roll about the pitch as if I'd shot both his legs off. When I offered him my hand to help pull him up he just stayed there. I couldn't believe it and told him to get up and stop messing about, so what does the referee do? He books me for ungentlemanly conduct!

When we came off at the end, we were all bubbling because we'd played so well and we knew that we were through to the quarter-finals, barring the biggest of nightmares. George sat down and said, 'Well played, lads! But, Wrighty, what were you doing getting yourself booked?' I could not believe what he was saying and I just laid into him. 'What the hell are you talking about? You were the one who said to help them up, and that's got me into trouble. If it wasn't for you, I would never have got booked.' That's when George started playing the old tactical card.

He left me out of the return leg in Belgium and, just my luck, Standard just capitulated from the first whistle and Arsenal won 7–0. All I could do was sit on the bench wondering just how many I would have got against a defence that bottled it from the first kick. The ridiculous thing was that by leaving me out of those sort of games, George probably just delayed the inevitable. If I'd got booked in the second game against Standard or the first match in the next round against Torino, then I would only have missed the first leg of a possible semi-final. Instead I had this yellow card hanging over my head like the sword of Damocles and low and behold, I got a second one in the semi-final.

George kept me out of the first game with Torino. He didn't tell me what he was going to do, he just called the team out and I wasn't in it. I wanted him to have a bit of respect for me and trust me to get on with a game instead of worrying about a booking. Instead he left me out and I missed the chance of playing in the Stadio Dell Alpi, one of the best grounds in Europe, on a major occasion.

But even without me the lads played magnificently to get a 0–0 draw which was as good a performance as smashing seven past the Belgians. Torino were a strong side who had some excellent players, especially in attack, but Tony and Steve proved just what a great pairing they are and were absolutely immense in that game, and put us in with a hope at Highbury. And it was Tony who made sure that we went through when he smacked in a header from about six yards out that the keeper didn't even sniff, let alone get a hand to. I was back in the side for that one, kept my nose clean and played really well, so at least there was nothing George could say to me after that except 'well done'.

We got lucky in the semi-final and pulled out Paris St Germain whom most people thought were the weakest team in the competition. That may have been true, but those were two of the toughest matches I have ever played in. The first leg was over there in the Parc des Princes, and anybody who ever says that French crowds lack passion wasn't there that night because, boy, those were some pumped-up Frenchmen! There were fire crackers going off, the drums were beating and it felt like we were entering a cauldron of noise.

But through all the games we'd been building up a really special team spirit, and there was a feeling in the camp that whatever was put in front of us, we could knock it down. I think George wanted that 'us against the world' kind of atmosphere because whenever a newspaper or television programme said that we couldn't do it, he'd be in like a flash: 'Did you see what they're saying about you, they don't think you're up to it, so just go out and show them.' Critics say that Arsenal always put up a lot of walls and don't trust anybody from the outside, which is not strictly true. What we do believe in is doing it for ourselves and not for anybody else, and if we're being written off, fair enough. All we have to do is point to our medals at the end of each season.

It was like that against PSG and that's why I was so excited to score the goal over there. Away goals are like gold dust, and as soon as the header went in you could sense the mood in the stadium was ready to turn against PSG and that the French fans didn't believe that their side could get themselves back in the game. David Ginola did admittedly level things up not long afterwards but there was no way we were ever going to be beaten that night, and a 1–1 draw was almost as good as a win because Fortress Highbury would not be breached.

If the Parc des Princes had been alive, then Highbury was like a mass of emotion, and for me that emotion was going to spill over in the worst possible way. We were playing well and creating a few chances, but the breaks weren't going for us and, I have to admit, I was getting frustrated. But that had absolutely nothing to do with what happened a few minutes before half-time. PSG were breaking out and I went across to try and cut the attack out. I went in for a tackle with some guy – to this day I can't exactly remember who it was – we collided and both went down. The crowd went silent for a second and then went crazy, because they saw the referee pulling out his card and that meant only one thing: I was out of the final.

My whole world crumbled in those few seconds. The tears started flowing and there was nothing I could do to stop them. I just wanted to get away from Highbury, away from football and away from the depression that had already grabbed me by the throat. The minutes up to the break were a blur and as soon as the referee blew for half-time I started crying again, and by the time I got to the dressing room I was just sobbing.

I know George was only being professional, but his mood and attitude just saw me hit boiling point. I came in and a few of the lads were trying to console me, but he cut through all that and said, 'Wrighty, f****** stop crying and grow up.' That was it, the red mist came down and I went ballistic. I was shouting and swearing at him, calling him every name under the sun, kicking out at everything and generally wanting to fight the world. He gave as good as he got, and I swear I don't know how it didn't end in punches. I just stormed into the showers, sobbing my heart out. I think Stewart Houston was coming in after me, but George shouted, 'Leave the little cry baby alone to have his tantrum, we've got a game to win.'

Again, I know in my heart he was right, but at the time it was about the lowest I'd felt in my whole life. Everything I'd worked for right back to the previous summer and the FA Cup Final had gone out of the window and I really didn't know how I was going to carry on. Perhaps George was right to react in the way he did, after all he had ten other players to consider, not just my feelings, but at the time I needed an arm around my shoulder, not a kick in the groin.

Finally Gary Lewin, our physio, came in and tried to lift me. He told me there was still something to play for, and that I had to do it for the other lads. Then Lee Dixon came in and he said one of the kindest things that anybody has ever said to me. It was simply, 'Wrighty, pull yourself together, the boys need you.' That made me realise just how selfish I had been to think the whole world revolved around me, that what it came down to was Arsenal Football Club, not Ian Wright. I know it sounds as if I acted like a spoiled brat, but I hope people can understand the emotions I was going through.

I did manage to get myself together for the second half, and I think knowing that this was my last chance in Europe this season made me even more determined. The fans were brilliant, they chanted my name throughout the second half and made me feel as if they were willing me to play well. When Kevin Campbell scored, the whole place erupted and suddenly there was the absolute belief that we were destined to be in Copenhagen.

You could hardly hear the final whistle, but as soon as it was over I just headed for the dressing rooms. It was the weirdest feeling, because on the one hand I was crushed beyond belief, but I also felt so up for the lads, so happy that they had got what they deserved. George was cool about everything afterwards – he just came up and thanked me for doing my bit to help Arsenal and said that he understood what I was going through. I'm not sure if anybody actually understood, but it was good of him to have a quiet word. I sat in the dressing room with all these thoughts buzzing around my head and it just occurred to me that I couldn't do a thing about it, so why was I worrying about it? That seemed to just click into my brain and I went into party animal mood. I must have drunk a couple of bottles of champagne, and that made me feel a bit better, and I also decided that the fans had to join in the celebrations. So there I was, stark naked, leaning out of the dressing room window into the street where all the fans were gathered, and I just sprayed so much champagne out of that window, it was unbelievable. One bloke was completely soaked, but all he did was continue to jump up and down, dance in the streets and sing idiotic songs about George Graham having a magic hat, or something like that.

I was well into it by then, and a few of the lads decided we'd go to a bar in the West End that stayed open till late and have a few drinks. But it didn't stop at a few, and by the end of the evening I was absolutely smashed, completely and utterly lagging, and all the pain disappeared until I woke up the next morning. A lot of the pain came back in the next couple of weeks, first against Chelsea and then against Villa when their fans were chanting 'Where's your final gone?' And then it was reported that I wouldn't get a medal so it was 'Where's your medal gone?' which hurt me because it made me realise just what a match I was missing. In the end though, I only had myself to blame and I suppose having a pop at George is easier than taking a long hard look at myself.

The build-up to the final against Parma was weird. There's nothing that I can ever compare it with because even in the FA Cup Final with Palace when I knew I wasn't going to start, at least I knew I would be involved at some stage. But for this one I was completely on the outside from the moment we started looking forward to the match. George and the boys did their best to get me involved and I joined in with all the banter, but there was nothing for me to grasp, nothing for me to focus on and that left a really empty feeling in the pit of my stomach. Thankfully, I've got a quite resilient character that can help me put a brave face on things and I wasn't going to mope around, bringing the rest of the boys down. In fact, the day before the final we trained in the stadium and I was really buzzing and enjoying the fact that at least I was there with the lads. It wasn't until they started doing set-pieces and pattern of play and I wasn't involved that I began to feel down. But I tell you, it was going to get a hell of a lot worse twenty-four hours later.

John Jensen was also missing the final after he got injured, and about an hour before kick-off we were both out on the pitch when the Arsenal vice-chairman, David Dein, came up to us and told us to go and give the fans a wave. We both walked over to the Arsenal supporters and the reception they gave us was tremendous. Needless to say, the old waterworks were turned on again and it really began to bother me.

I think that if Arsenal had lost, then I would never have been able to forgive myself. I would never have been able to look the rest of the boys straight in the eye because I would have felt as if I had let them down so badly, and I honestly felt frightened that we were going to lose. You only had to look at that Parma side to see why: the names of their world-class players just tripped off the tongue ... Brolin, Zola, Asprilla. They were the favourites, and rightly so, but I don't think they had an ounce of the belief that we had in ourselves.

When they hit the post early on, I don't know if it was God smiling on us or just warning us as to what Parma could really do. But as the game wore on, you could see the boys just swelling with confidence and when Alan Smith turned and shot and the ball sailed in, then I knew that was it, Parma were never getting back. Words can't describe how proud I was of every one of our players. The defence was brilliant, they snuffed out all the so-called Italian big guns; the midfield worked like crazy; and up front Kevin Campbell and Alan Smith ('Smudger') were fantastic. Smudger was the perfect hero for that night because he summed up everything that Arsenal stood for at the time: he was honest, not interested in personal glory and just loved playing football for the club. I was appalled at the start of last season when he had to pack the game in through injury.

But even while the lads were celebrating, they still knew what it meant to me not to have played. At the time, it didn't look as if UEFA were handing out medals to anybody who didn't actually play in the final, so I would have missed out. Paul Dickov, who hadn't been involved until the actual final, came up to me and offered me his medal because he said I deserved it more. I couldn't believe what he was actually doing, it was an incredible gesture, but I said, 'No man, you've got to keep it. It's a blinding gesture but you can't give that away. Whatever happens in your career, you've got a Cup Winners' Cup medal and you deserve it and you've got to treasure it.' And to be fair, for that ninety minutes I didn't deserve a medal because I wasn't eligible for that game. But over the course of the season, I think I deserved one for what I did. Fortunately, UEFA came up trumps and now that medal has just about pride of place in my collection.

The following season we had to defend that cup and I made it my ambition not to get a booking in the whole competition, and I was as good as my word. I felt good, I felt confident and I felt as if this was the season where people would really have to look at me in Europe and realise that I meant business. When you also consider what went on that season, how the club was almost torn apart by the whole George Graham situation and the problems that Merse faced, it was just an incredible feat to get back to the final.

For me, something just clicked into place as far as goals were concerned. Right from the first game against Nicosia in Cyprus, I was in the groove, feeling on the mark and knowing that I was the man, the one that Europe was going to be talking about. I got one in Cyprus and two more at Highbury in the return leg before we went over to Denmark to play Brondby, where I scored again and got a penalty at home as we won 4–3 on aggregate.

The only European game I didn't score in was the Super Cup against AC Milan. They held us 0–0 at our place and then beat us 2–0 over in the San Siro. What a place that is, and I really thought I had something to remember the match for when I 'scored' but the referee decided that I was offside, even though the TV replays show I was onside by about two yards. That was quite a bad time for the club because the revelations about George had broken and he was under incredible pressure, though you wouldn't know it to look back at those days. The only thing that lifted us was the fact that Merse was out of the rehabilitation clinic and back in the side. He played the whole game in Milan and I don't think I've ever been as glad to see somebody back as I was when Merse appeared on the scene again.

Milan gave us a footballing lesson and I don't think I've played against better defenders anywhere in the world than Franco Baresi and Paolo Maldini. Even Tony Adams and Steve Bould, who aren't exactly the worse pair of defenders around, said that the understanding Milan had was better than any other team in the world, so I felt a less disappointed about not getting on the scoresheet.

But when it mattered, I could come up with the goods. By the time we met Auxerre in the quarter-finals, George had been sacked, Stewart Houston was in charge and the eyes of the world were on us. Again that seemed to lift us in a strange way and we had to show everybody that whatever had gone on off the pitch, the players weren't going to suffer through it. I've got to say, I think Auxerre were the toughest team we played in either of the two seasons. They were physically intimidating, they were organised and they had the look about them that told you they meant business. I was getting used to the European way of marking because I'd been kicked from pillar to post everywhere from Poland to Cyprus so I knew roughly what to expect. Yet these guys took it to another dimension. At times it felt as if the geezer marking me was physically attached at the hip because every run I made, every turn, every shimmy, he was stuck to me like a leech. He battered me all night long in that first game at Highbury and how I managed to get a yard on him to score, I don't think I'll ever know.

Everybody knew that a 1–1 draw with them at Highbury was a poor result and, from the way they played, we had our work cut out in France. But the game proved to me that God had blessed me, that if I believed in Him, then He would always help me out and be at my side. Looking back on the match now, I still swear that He was with me through every step of the game, and scoring a goal was my way of thanking Him for all the assistance He has given to me through my life. I knew as soon as I picked up the ball that I was meant to score. I knew the goalkeeper was too far off his line and I knew I had to get my shot over and across him, but even if he had been perfectly positioned, then I don't think he would have been allowed to save it. From the moment the ball left my foot I knew it was going in and I was off and away.

If you look at the video of me celebrating, it wasn't my usual style. I just went down on my knees and looked up to heaven because I knew that God had helped me and I knew that I had to thank Him. It was one of the most special goals I have ever scored, not because it was spectacular, not because it won us the tie but because it came from Him. Whenever I see that goal, I always get a strange feeling because it never seems to be me scoring it: I always feel detached from it, as if I'm watching a stranger score.

Now people were really starting to get that old familiar buzz. Our league form was useless, there was virtually a new scandal every day involving the club, and we didn't have a manager, just somebody filling in while the board made up their mind what they were going to do. But in Europe, on the pitch where it mattered, nothing was stopping us, and even a semi-final against Sampdoria didn't seem as daunting as it might have for any other side.

But just as we were getting into our stride, we did our best to chuck it all away in a crazy game with Sampdoria at Highbury. We were strolling it, the Italians couldn't cope with Steve Bould from set-pieces and he helped himself to a couple of goals. Sampdoria got one back but I helped stop the panic when I got our third, yet even when that one went in, I still had the horrible feeling that they were going to have the final say. And I was exactly right when they got a second away goal late on to set up an incredible match in Genoa.

David Platt told me that the Sampdoria lads were all desperate to stop me scoring at their place because they felt if they closed me out, then Arsenal would struggle. That's why there was so much satisfaction for me to get one over there, to shake off players like Ricardo Ferri and Pietro Viechewod and get in front from a corner and put the ball in the back of the net. If Auxerre was the most spectacular goal of that run, then the one against Sampdoria meant the most. Luckily for me though, that goal was overshadowed by David Seaman in the penalty shoot-out. I'd got a whack in the second half and could hardly move, so I had to come off, but by that time I'd lost all sense of what was going on in the game. I was upset and frustrated that I'd had to come off. I was gutted because I'd lost count of the score and thought we were going out, and I was on the brink of tears all the time. Then when Stefan Schwarz scored with about thirty seconds to go, I lost control – I was grabbing people, sobbing with joy, and that was before the penalty kicks.

Funnily enough I felt calm despite all the tension of penalties because I knew we had big Dave and I knew that he was the king of the spot-kick situation. Two seasons before against Millwall in the League Cup he'd got us through single-handedly in the penalties and I knew he could do it again. When he stopped shot after shot and the Sampdoria players were losing their bottle, I couldn't help but smile to myself because the big man had done it again. At the end, it was what football was all about to me. I felt invincible, that nothing could stop me. I ran to the fans and we connected, we knew that this was something special, that out of adversity Arsenal had done it yet again.

I really felt our name was on the cup that year and, to be honest, I looked at Zaragoza and they didn't compare to the Parma side we had beaten the year before, and they hadn't beaten the quality of opponents we had to get to the final. It wasn't a case of disrespecting them, I just didn't have that fear that I had against Parma. The only player I thought was trouble was the Argentinian kid, Esnaider. I felt that he could cause us some problems from all the tapes I had seen of him. He did turn out to be the danger man because he scored an absolutely magnificent goal. He drilled it in on the volley from about thirty yards and, to be fair, Dave didn't stand a chance with it. We got back into it thanks to John Hartson, and for ten minutes we absolutely blitzed them, and Merse had a header that he really should have scored with. If that had gone in, then we would have coasted it.

But when the game went into extra-time, I couldn't see either side scoring and penalties were the only way the game was going to be decided. That was until Nayim ripped my heart out. When I think back on it, defeat in that game was easier to take because we had lost to such an outstanding piece of individual skill that you couldn't do anything but take your hat off to the guy.

There was just a few seconds to go, he was on the halfway line but still had the bottle to go for the shot, and he judged it to perfection. I wasn't saying that at the time because if I'd have come across him at any time that following week, he would have got chinned, no problem, and I'm sure Dave would have done the same! If the only thing I had done in that game was to score that Nayim goal, I would have been the proudest man in the world. And he scored it in the last thirty seconds of a final! A player only ever dreams of beating the keeper from the halfway line, and even if you attempt it what are the odds on you executing it? When the ball nestled in the back of our net, the first thought was disappointment that we'd lost, but when the realisation set in, all I could think of was: 'What a fabulous goal!'. If you're going to lose, then I'd rather lose like that: it's got to be better than being the person who misses a penalty to lose the final. The more you think about it as an amazing piece of skill and talent all coming together in a split second, the easier it is to accept defeat. That goal was worthy of winning any game, a World Cup, anything. I can deal with it now, and if Nayim ever reads this, good luck and well played, ultimate respect.

The person whom I felt most for was Dave. He just sat there wondering what had happened, but, for perhaps the only time in history, you couldn't blame a keeper for being beaten from that far out, there was absolutely nothing he could do. It must be difficult for Dave to live with it, though, because that's the one people will always bring up, not the incredible saves he makes week after week, but that one goal. I was out with him and his wife in the West End having a quiet drink when some geezer goaded him with 'Nayim from the halfway line', so I just turned round to the fellow and told him to clear off. It's bad enough Dave having it every Saturday, he doesn't need it from punters on a night out, it's too much.

13
Total Respect
for George

George Graham made me the player that I am today. Without him, I would never have achieved half of what I have in football and that is why I will defend him to my dying day. And it's not just me that he made, he made Arsenal Football Club great again as well, by restoring them to the top of the English game. I'm not interested in what he did off the pitch. All I care about is the medals that he helped put in my collection because, without him, my trophy cupboard would be a pretty bare place, I can tell you.

I'm not saying that he and I were best of mates while he was at Highbury; in fact we had some blazing rows and huge bust-ups that a lot of the players couldn't believe. But at the end of the day, I respected that man and I knew he was one of the greatest managers there has ever been. You only have to look at his record in the nine seasons he was at Arsenal to see that he's up there with the likes of Brian Clough, Bill Shankly, Bob Paisley and Alex Ferguson. We might have argued the toss and slaughtered each other, but we both had that respect and I don't think I'll ever work with anybody like him again.

The Arsenal boys always used to call me and Tony Adams 'Sons of George' because basically they reckoned we could get away with anything and he wouldn't bat an eyelid, but they weren't on the end of anything like the dressing-downs he used to give me. If they had been, then the old 'Son of George' thing would have gone out of the window pretty quickly.

I didn't know the guy at all until I signed for Arsenal. We'd never met socially or even passed the time of day, although David Rocastle always told me that George fancied me as a player and would like to bring me to Highbury. He fancied me so much that he didn't even bother turning up when I signed, he was too busy playing golf! But even if I didn't know him, I knew about his reputation and that frightened the life out of me.

Any one of my managers will tell you that I can be a handful at times. I tend to sulk if things aren't going right for me, but if I'm 'up' then I can be hyper and a bit of a pain. I was worried because I didn't know if George could accept that, what with him being a strict disciplinarian with a temper that scared even senior professionals at times. In my first training session, I kept myself to myself, didn't say much and just got on with whatever he told us to do and everything seemed cool. He welcomed me to the club, told me that all he wanted me to do was play my natural game and score goals and everything would be sweet.

The next day we played up at Leicester and at half-time things weren't going very well and we were struggling desperately. I was dreading his team talk because I could see that he was furious with us. Straight away he ripped into our defence, accusing them of being sloppy, giving too much away and really gave them a hard time. Suddenly Steve Bould turned round and just said, 'F*** off, George, it's not just the defence who are crap.'

I couldn't believe it. This was George Graham, the manager of Arsenal, one of the top managers around – you didn't answer him back, let alone tell him to f*** off! But suddenly Lee Dixon joined in and the three of them had a right set-to.

My chin must have hit the floor – I just sat there staring around the dressing room wondering what the hell was going on.

It was then that I realised that George wasn't that aloof figure whom you couldn't talk to, he was down to earth, genuine and cared so passionately about Arsenal that it physically hurt him if things weren't going right. And if things weren't going right, then you soon found out about it.

I thought my first season was going pretty well: I was scoring goals regularly, I'd struck up a great understanding with the rest of the boys and I was flying. But to listen to George at half-time, full-time or on the training ground, you'd think I was some two-bob carthorse who couldn't kick a ball straight, let alone play for Arsenal. I've lost count of the number of times he'd come in at half-time and say, 'Defence – superb; midfield – you're working well, keep it up. But up front – what the f*** is going on? What are you doing?' Then he would castigate me and Kevin or Smudger for the rest of the break.

I learned early on that I had to give as good as I got back, otherwise I'd be a nervous wreck and invariably it would end up in a slanging match. But George knew exactly what he was doing because every time I would go out for the second half I was so pumped up trying to stuff those words down his throat that my game would improve by at least 10 per cent. Now I know that slippery Scottish strategist was conning me all the time. He knew what buttons to press with me and he pressed them every time, so I've got to hold my hands up and say he was right to hammer me, although it sticks in my throat even now!

With George it was never a personal thing but was always done on a purely football level. If he thought you were useless or cheating or just not pulling your weight, he told you so and, even though it hurt at the time, you knew it would be forgotten the next day. I've come into training on a Monday after he's had a go at me on the Saturday, knowing that he was going to pull me up at some time. He'd start off by smiling and saying, 'How are you doing this morning?' and get on with the session. There would be no bitterness, no snide remarks and no repeat of the weekend, but when we were alone in his office he would try to explain why he was having a go. I'd sit there, take it and try to explain my point of view. When you're angry, you say things in the heat of the moment, not to be disrespectful, but just to try and get your opinion over. He knew that, accepted it, and that's what won him the respect of virtually every Arsenal player I've ever known.

Often I would apologise in front of all the boys for what I might have said to George. It would be a case of standing up, holding my hands up and just giving it an honest apology. George would sometimes pull me up and say that I didn't have to apologise, but I wanted the lads to know that it was just heat of the moment, that I wasn't disrespecting him, and that the rest of the team shouldn't disrespect him. That's one of the major differences between George and Bruce Rioch. With George there was never anything psychological: it was black or white, right or wrong, whereas Bruce is pretty intense in the mind games and I'm still trying to find my feet with him and work it out.

George often used to say to me, 'Ian, never let what goes on during a match colour what you think off the pitch. If I carried on rows then I wouldn't speak to a single player for the rest of the week. It's all business, son, nothing but business, so when the business side of things is over, relax and enjoy life.' That's something that has stuck with me and I try to carry it out. When I'm on the pitch, it's deadly serious, life and death even. But as soon as that final whistle is blown, then I'm ready to forget all about football and get on with my life. George taught me an invaluable lesson and I hope I never forget it.

George and I may have been completely different characters, but he knew what made me tick. He realised that I played by instinct, that I wanted to try different things all the time, and he encouraged me. A lot of managers might have tried to knock the maverick side of my game out of me, and get me to fit more into a team pattern, but George just told me to trust what I believed in and go for it. He may have hated the way I got into trouble on the pitch, but he always insisted that I keep the fire in my belly because he realised that, without it, I was only half the player. It hurts me when I'm not playing well and it hurts me when I lose, and he once told me that he wished a few more professional footballers felt that much pain when things weren't going right.

And there was never any judgement of what you might get up to off the pitch. I don't think George dares criticise anybody for the lifestyle they lead, because in his day he was just about one of the biggest football playboys around. I've seen pictures of him strolling down the King's Road in his Chelsea and Arsenal days, opening boutiques and being quite the man-about-town with the rest of the chaps, so he couldn't complain if some of us followed suit.

People accused him of showing too much loyalty towards players, but how can that be a bad thing? We knew if we stepped out of line away from the club, then we were going to get hammered; it was just that it was purely behind closed doors and the press never got to hear about it. Because they didn't hear about it, they thought we were getting away with blue murder, which is absolute rubbish because anybody who knows George's standards of discipline knows that he would never accept anything out of order. But once you'd been punished, that was it, there would be no recriminations.

Sometimes I thought that he was a lucky manager. He was also one of the greatest tacticians and some of the chances he took with players came off with a bit of good luck. He would throw in somebody like Ian Selley, even though he was

187

untried, and Ian would come good. George played Stevie Morrow in the League Cup Final when a lot of critics couldn't understand why he did it, then Stevie pops up to score the winner. The best example is Paul Davis. George was absolutely livid that 'Davvo' had done a piece in the papers, after he got a testimonial, criticising the way that George's teams played, that they didn't pass the ball around enough for his liking. I don't think that I've ever seen George so angry over a newspaper article, because it seemed like a betrayal. 'Davvo' was out of the side for eighteen months, but when George needed him, Paul was back and playing at Wembley three times after being stuck in the reserves for a lifetime.

George never lost the players as some people have claimed: he made too many Arsenal players rich, he brought too many youth team players through and made them into internationals and he helped fill up too many trophy cabinets for any of us to turn our back on him. Having said that, you could sense things turning stale in that last season and perhaps the time was right for him to bow out gracefully. Our league form was dreadful and the three cup wins of the past two seasons had papered over a lot of cracks. George tried to buy players like Roy Keane and Chris Sutton but they just weren't available at the sort of price the club was willing to shell out or the wages they were willing to pay.

If everything had gone according to plan, I think George would have said, 'Right, I've gone as far as I can with the club. It's time to leave while things are still reasonably good.' The club could then have thanked him for his services, given him a nice fat testimonial and everybody would have been sweet. Instead he went out in the worst possible way.

I'm not going to get into the rights and wrongs of what he did because I don't know enough about it. The only thing I will say is that if you sat down 99 per cent of the people in this country and opened a briefcase containing two hundred grand in £50 notes, how many of us would say, 'Take that away, I'm not interested'? I'll tell you, not many. If there's a man in Britain who can honestly say that he wouldn't be tempted to take that, especially if they were told it was a gift, I'll lick his boots. Then I'd take him out for a drink and try to find out what makes him tick, because it's that sort of substance of character that I admire.

There had been some whispers going on at Arsenal for a couple of weeks in November 1994 before the story actually broke that George had taken over £200,000 from the transfer of John Jensen and Pal Lydersen. None of the players seemed too interested, because that's all we thought they were – whispers and rumours – and as far as we were concerned it didn't involve any of us. Then when the story actually came out in one of the Sunday papers, I just thought that it was purely paper talk, that George and the club would come out with a statement and it would all be cleared up. But then even more stories were coming out and the whole thing was growing every day. That's when we started making jokes, saying that the boss was taking a back-hander if he wasn't out for training in time or was late for a team meeting. We still weren't that bothered, because we felt it would all blow over before too long, and anyway there couldn't be too much wrong because George just acted as if nothing had even been said.

He didn't miss a training session, he didn't show any emotion when there were herds of reporters and photographers waiting for him wherever he went, and he certainly didn't take us all to one side and explain what was going on. Instead, he was the usual George – laughing, joking, slaughtering people and generally getting on with life. I'm not sure how he did it and how he managed it. Perhaps football was the only thing in his life keeping him steady, or perhaps he was trying to shield the players from all the hassle. Whatever it was, we never saw any other side of him but

George the football manager, and that was exactly the way it had to be. I had people asking me constantly what was going on, but I could honestly say that I knew absolutely nothing at all.

I'm ashamed to say it now, but there were times when he was having a go at me, that I thought to myself, 'I hope you're guilty.' It doesn't give me any great pleasure to reveal that, because I look at myself now and just wonder how I could have stooped so low as to wish that on anybody, especially George. All I will say is that again it was in the heat of the moment and if you're reading this, George, I'm sorry, mate. I desperately wish I could take back all those thoughts.

As the whole affair dragged on, I just wondered why the Arsenal board hadn't either sacked him right at the start or come out with a statement that gave George their full backing until any investigation proved otherwise. That question has been troubling me for a long time. I think we could all have understood it if George had been booted out straight away, and although it would have been bloody difficult to accept, we would have said, 'OK, George is gone, let's just get on with life.' But as it was, we didn't know what was going to be happening next week, next month or next year.

I personally believe that's what hurt George the most – he thought the club was going to back him to the hilt. I went on Channel 4 television's 'The Word' and said if the board were going to sack George, they should go on and do it instead of letting him die a slow, lingering death. I got into bother with the club over that. But if a racehorse breaks his leg, you don't let him carry on running, you shoot it there and then, and that's what should have happened with George. What was even more confusing was that just before Arsenal sacked him, they allowed him to go and spend almost £6 million on Glenn Helder, John Hartson and Chris Kiwomya.

There are all sorts of theories still going round Highbury that try and explain what happened to George. People were saying that he'd got too big for the club, that he was more powerful than the directors and that a few people on the board resented it and that there was a conspiracy to get rid of him. I don't really know myself, but that theory has a ring of truth to it.

I would describe myself and George as good friends and when it seemed clear that the allegations weren't going away, I went up to him and asked what the hell was going on and whether he was going to be here for much longer. He just shrugged his shoulders and said that he didn't know, that he was waiting to find out himself. That was the closest I or any of the other players came to raising the subject with him.

When George was eventually sacked, it was all done in two minutes flat: clear your desk and get out and don't ever darken our door again. That was just a desperate day for me. I read it on teletext and I was completely devastated: I couldn't believe that he was really gone, that George wasn't going to be around at Arsenal any more. For the next week or so, I just expected the ghost of George to come striding out onto the training pitch with a big smile on his face and tell us that it was all a huge mistake and that everything was going to be all right. But he was sacked on the morning of our match with Nottingham Forest. The day before, George had come into training as usual, we'd worked on set plays and pattern of play as usual, and we all left looking forward to the game. Twenty-four hours later, the bomb was dropped.

We beat Forest, but every single one of us was still shell-shocked at the news and I don't think there was one player who could quite honestly believe what had happened that day.

People have asked me if there was an added pressure after George had been sacked, but it wasn't so much a case of pressure, more that we were in the spotlight even more than before. The pressure was to get things turned around with or without George because we were in real danger of getting dragged into a relegation battle. All right, we were still in the European Cup Winners' Cup but everybody could see that things weren't exactly going well, and if anybody thought that there was going to be a sudden transformation under Stewart Houston, then they were kidding themselves. We'd been rubbish all season, so how the hell were we suddenly going to go on a blistering run that would shoot us up the league?

I felt sorry for Stewart, but I honestly don't know what he was doing in those first few weeks he was in charge. I suppose he was under a lot of pressure because he obviously wanted the job full-time and the board didn't exactly help him by saying that they would review the job in the summer, so he was in limbo. I don't know if he wanted to prove that he was his own man and that he was strong enough to take the job, but I think I got used as a sacrifice. I'll admit I wasn't playing well but I still felt as if I was doing enough to warrant a place, but Stewart didn't.

He called me in after a couple of games and asked me how I thought it was going. We talked and I knew he was building up for something because he kept mentioning changes and trying a few different things. I made it easy for him. I said, 'Are you going to drop me?' And he said, 'Well, I think I'm going to have to.' 'That's fine,' I said, 'just f****** well do it. I won't go bleating to the papers about it, saying that I want to leave. I would never demean myself like that. But I'm telling you one thing, you're making a massive mistake.'

With that I was out of the team for the game against Blackburn, although he brought me back against Auxerre a week or so later. I scored and he never left me out again. Looking back, I don't know whether Stewart was just trying to flex his muscles to show the lads and the board that he was strong enough to be manager and take big decisions, but whatever it was, it left a nasty taste in my mouth and it was quite a long time before we were back on good terms.

The rest of that season was a terrible, terrible time for the club except for the European Cup Winners' Cup Final, and even that turned into a nightmare thanks to Nayim. Thankfully we were safe in the league by that time – although it was only two matches before the end of the season that we could say that – but it would have been nice to have won the cup, just so that people could have something positive to say about Arsenal instead of bringing up all the dreadful things that had happened. There was still a stigma attached to the club because of the George Graham affair, and if we could have won the cup it would have shown outsiders that the players hadn't been affected by everything that had gone on off the pitch. I suppose the shadow hanging over the club was caused by the fact that there had been no decision by the FA on whether they considered George guilty or not. That dragged into the summer and just delayed the agony for him. When they did find him guilty and banned him for a year in June 1995, I suppose there was a sense of relief that it was all over and that everybody connected with the club could turn over a new leaf and start afresh.

I still keep in touch with George, although in the days after he was sacked there were some sticky moments. We went out for an Italian meal in Islington just to sit down, catch up with what was going on and generally talk about football. But as we sat down we noticed that the Arsenal vice-chairman David Dein was sitting with his brother about three tables down from us. For a moment I didn't know what to do. I felt very uncomfortable because I knew how it might look, but I can honestly say that George and I were just out as old friends. To be fair, David Dein was really cool about it and took it at face value, but for a moment I was very worried.

That's the problem when people are thought to be tainted: others expect you to stick the knife in straight away. I would never, ever do that as far as George is concerned. I will never denounce him for what he has done. People ask why he did it when he was earning a good wage as manager of Arsenal. Maybe it was for the same reason as the person who doesn't stop earning money just because they've become a millionaire. It's a basic human instinct. George thought the money was a gift, so he accepted it.

To wipe away all traces of George from Highbury is hypocritical. You can't just take down all the pictures of him around the place and pretend that he didn't exist, because you'd have to forget about all the trophies that he won and all the money that he made for the club. It's all very well saying that the club has got to move on, it's got to look to the future, but you just can't wipe away the past as if it never happened. Admittedly, as far as Arsenal are concerned, George was wrong to take the backhander, but does that suddenly make him a figure of hatred? I can understand them not using his voice in the club museum because there's a new manager now, but there's no way that you can wipe away the legend.

By the time this book is published, he might very well be in a new job. In fact I would say that it's a racing certainty that he will be back in work, because those in football aren't stupid – they know a class act when they see one. I don't see why George shouldn't become one of the top managers in the country and build a new team that could go on to dominate as Arsenal did. He's done his time, and now I think he'll be refreshed and ready to go for it again, and I know he's looking forward to the challenge because he still feels there's a lot for him to prove.

We still talk and I am always asking his advice and picking his brains because I respect his views. He talks so much sense, he's got so much experience and he knows exactly what makes footballers tick and clubs run properly. Without him I know that I would never have achieved half of what I have done in football, because when I left Palace for Arsenal

I was still raw and rough round the edges. George looked at me and decided that he wanted to keep some of those rough edges and add a few more strings to my bow as well. He was always there to support me when things weren't going right, he backed me 100 per cent when people tried to blacken my name or tarnish my reputation and he was always there if I had a problem that I needed sorting out.

It's all too easy for players to say they've got the club running through their veins because the bottom line with players is that they'll get on with life whatever team they play for. But as far as George was concerned, Arsenal was so much a part of him that it left a massive hole when it was ripped away, and it is a hole that I don't think will ever be really filled again.

I hope that whatever George Graham does in life, he will be successful at it. One thing's for sure – I'll always have total respect for him.

14
My Mates

While the whole George Graham thing was going on, another scandal hit Arsenal, and this time it was one that became personal. Everybody knew that Paul Merson liked a drink and was well into gambling, but not one person at the club realised the depth of his problems. I don't even think that his wife, Lorraine, knew just how bad things had got for him. The only person who knew just what sort of hell he was going through was Merse himself, and to carry that burden around for as long as he did, I just don't know how he got on with life, let alone kept playing football.

It's so refreshing to speak to him now because he's so open about all his problems, but when he sits down and tells you that there were times when he was in his car and all he wanted to do was drive it into a wall or a tree and end everything, that's when you realise just what a complete and utter nightmare he was living every day of his life. When I look at him now and think what he used to be like, I know that no matter how hard the treatment might have been for him, it was worth every second of agony because he's a completely new person.

Before, you could not get his attention for more than a minute. It was always the horses or the dogs and betting, betting, betting. We used to go to a hotel before an away game, get there about 12.30 for some lunch and leave at 5.30 at the latest. In that time Merse would have spent £70 on phone calls to bookies, no problem. He would be phoning America and places like that, just to get results of races or American football matches, anything that he could have a gamble on.

But nobody at the club knew just how bad his drinking had got. To me, when Merse had a drink he became the life and soul of the party, he'd do stupid things and he'd make me laugh. When he was out with the lads though, he never appeared any different to the rest of us, because we'd all be drinking, getting a bit pissed and just relaxing. I think it was the drinking away from us that was the problem. We didn't very often go out in a big crowd so nobody knew exactly what he was doing away from the Arsenal lads. I like a drink now and again, but it doesn't take too much to get me drunk, and most of the time I know when to call it a day. But Merse couldn't stop drinking until he was absolutely paralytic and couldn't physically have another drop. To me, that was the most frightening thing he ever told me.

Although now I know that he was an alcoholic, he also got set up badly a few times. Merse, Paul Ince and I were at the BRIT Awards a few years back, and we were all having a drink when suddenly a girl who works in the media came up and just plonked a crate of Budweisers next to Paul's chair just so that it made a great story in the gossip columns the next day. The report said that Lorraine was so disgusted with his drinking that she stormed out. What actually happened was that some bird stuck her tongue down Merse's throat, Lorraine quite rightly got the hump and they left together.

I don't think he realised what he was starting when he did the double-handed drinking gesture after we'd won the Coca Cola Cup. It was just copying Gazza who'd done it when Spurs beat Arsenal in the semi-final, but straight away everybody associated it with Merse. If he ever got into any scrapes off the pitch, that photo would appear in the papers and people immediately thought, 'Merson the piss-head.' It was those sort of pictures and those sort of reports that started going around and everywhere we went, punters would come up and say, 'Merse likes a drink doesn't he?' when none of them had ever met him, let alone been out in his company. The pressure was building on him and I suppose he thought he had to do something before he cracked.

When he decided to confess in a newspaper, he told me and said that he was going away for a few days. I just wished him all the best, but I had no idea what was going to be in the article. I thought he was going to talk about money problems that he had through gambling or even something about his drinking, but I could never have guessed that he was going to admit to taking cocaine. Merse says that he wasn't hooked on coke, that he only tried it a few times, but I suppose that's what makes the sensational headlines. His real problems were drink and gambling, and he says now that if he had not had treatment when he did, then he would be dead by now. That sounds dramatic when you read it but he tells it in such a matter-of-fact way that it somehow hits home even more.

The first person I thought of when I read the pieces that Paul did was Lorraine. I couldn't imagine what she had been through because, although I knew she was a brilliant woman, I couldn't understand how she had put up with everything that went along with having a husband who is an alcoholic and a compulsive gambler. When everything had come out, I thought 'Great, now they can start putting their lives back together.' But the newspapers found some slag who said she'd been with Paul, and it just blew it all open again. It was exactly what they didn't need, and to make matters worse, the paper put a line in asking anybody else who'd been with Merse to phone this number. How can that be right? How can that be anything but obscene? It's just carving another huge chunk of his life out and throwing it to the public.

Unlike the George Graham affair, Merse's problems did affect the lads and it hit us badly. Paul was our mate and we didn't like to see him suffering and that rather put a cloud over the whole squad because Merse was having such a bad time. When it was announced that he would be going into a rehabilitation clinic, I was glad on the one hand but so worried on the other. I was pleased that he was going to get the treatment that he needed, but he was so fragile at that time that I didn't know whether he could actually handle it. I honestly didn't know whether he would come through it and come back to Arsenal.

I think every single one of the lads must have spoken to him or gone to see him at the clinic in Southampton. Every day we'd all ask how he was getting on, when he was coming out and was he all right. Gary Lewin used to see him regularly because he'd help keep him fit while he was in the clinic, and Gary could see positive signs in Paul, knew that he was battling through it, although he obviously knew how much mental pain Merse was struggling with. There was something about the clinic that frightened me and I didn't actually go down to visit Merse. It was strange, but I didn't feel I could handle seeing him face to face, knowing what he'd been through. I thought I might break down and that wasn't going to be the best thing for Paul: he needed somebody who would be strong for him. But we spoke regularly on the phone and that was enough to open my eyes. He told me that although he had bad problems, there were people alongside him that were ten times worse, people who were just one step away from ending it all, or who had been in prison because of their addictions or living rough as down-and-outs.

Deborah and I broke down ourselves when he came out of the clinic and cried at a televised press conference. Anybody who knows Paul will tell you he is such a proud person, and it's impossible to believe that he would actually cry on TV.

He said afterwards that he cried so much in the clinic through all the treatments that he didn't think there were any tears left, but when he realised what he'd been through, they just came gushing out.

The whole experience has made Paul into one of the strongest people I know and suddenly people are beginning to lean on him. A lot of the lads ask his advice on drinking and gambling because he hit rock bottom and has come back. He'll go off to his meetings when we're away and then come back and talk about what went on there, and people will talk about the problems that they're having, and you have to say that it's a great thing to be able to share what's inside you. He admits that he still fancies a drink every day, but he says that he can handle it because he's seen where it leads. He's the only one that knows it in his heart whether he will or not, but I have a gut feeling that he will never drink again. He's realised the love that he has for Lorraine and his three boys and he doesn't want to chuck that all away for the sake of a drink or a flutter on the horses.

What really makes me feel strongly towards him is that he can actually be out with the lads while they're drinking and handle it. If it was me, I'd be so scared of the temptation that I would just lock myself away from people who were having a drink, but Merse is just so cool about it. When we're out, the boys do look after Merse because there are some cruel people around who want to spike his drinks. But if we're all together nobody can buy Merse a drink without Tony Adams or Steve Bould, his bodyguards if you like, tasting it first.

Paul can also laugh about his problems. We were at Planet Hollywood not so long ago and a girl made it perfectly clear that she fancied him and kept saying how much she admired what he had done and been through. Merse just looked at me, shook his head and said, 'Sorry darling, but you're about two years too late,' and then just fell about laughing because he realised just how easy it would have been for him to have cracked a couple of years back. He's a funny guy, and he just makes me die when we're out. He'll walk past me and shout over his shoulder, 'You're drinking too much!' Or if I say, 'Merse, I'm going to drink this beer through a straw, what do you reckon?' he'll just shake his head, get that little grin on his face and say, 'Wrighty, bad idea.' Last season, Bruce Rioch bought champagne whenever it was one of our birthdays and Merse just said, 'Jesus, why couldn't this have happened while I was on the drink? A great idea like this and I can't join in!'

Merse let me read chapters of his book before it was published and, although I felt for him, I learned that Lorraine was the one who went through everything as well. I like Lorraine, she's so strong, and it's obvious that she has so much love for Paul. I'm glad that they're together and getting things straightened out because they're a great family. I love his three kids, Ben, Charlie and Sam, and I just hope and pray that the five of them never have to go through anything like that ever again.

When we go away from home, Tony Adams, Merse and I don't half get some abuse, but what Paul has to handle is unbelievable. You get idiots like the fan at Middlesbrough last season who stood outside the coach while we were waiting to leave the stadium, pretending to sniff up lines of coke off his hand right in front of Merse. Then he pointed at me and started pretending to take a puff on a joint or something. What can you do with idiots like that? All you can do is laugh at them, but that just wound this guy up even more and he started screaming for us to get off the coach and start a fight. Then there are the fools who make jokes to Merse during a game about sniffing up the goal-line, or if makes a mistake they tell him to go and get a drink and maybe he'll play better. It's incredible, but Merse just laughs at the ignorant fools and I'm pleased that he can handle it and hit back by playing well now.

Graham Taylor was almost as bad as those who shouted from the stands. Merse and I were in the England squad in America to play against Germany in a friendly match and Taylor was going through the line-up. He started reeling off the names, and what he expected from each player, and when he got to Paul he said, 'I want Merse to get in and around the box, but unless I put a pint of beer in the six yard box, then there's no chance.' He must have thought he was being funny, but all the lads just looked at each other and thought, 'What an imbecile.'

Merse is a shining light now. He told me that he has an addictive personality and that he can get hooked on anything, so now he's into fitness training and he's in great shape right now. He's one of those guys who is naturally talented at all sports, tennis, snooker, the lot. I just want to get him over to the house now that I've got my snooker room and table and see if he's still the business or whether I'm the champion now.

I've been so lucky in my career as a footballer to have played and worked alongside some of the strongest characters and personalities around. Everybody talks about the strength of spirit in the Arsenal team, but that's purely down to the strength of character amongst the players, and there isn't anybody who stands for that more than Tony Adams.

He's a colossus, the sort of guy you want alongside and not playing against. I used to dread playing against Arsenal when I was with Palace because I knew that Tony would make me look bad. I had the speed to get away from most defenders, but his positional sense was so good that every time I made a run he'd be there, and a great big size 10 would boot me or the ball or both into orbit.

Tony is a real man's man. He works hard, he plays hard and he does everything 100 per cent, and if you aren't doing it to the same level, then he'll get behind you and make you want to do it. The biggest compliment I can pay to Tony is that he lifts me and motivates me more than any manager because if he thinks I've done something well, he'll tell me, and I know there's no bullshit. All he says to me before a match is for me to make runs, work hard and he knows the goals will come. Sometimes in training the ball will be bouncing off me or my touch is useless and Tony will shout, 'Don't worry Wrighty, just score goals and you'll do for me,' and that will give me such a buzz.

The bloke is a brilliant captain. He doesn't frighten me like Jim Cannon used to do at Palace, where I spent all my time trying to please him just so that he would say something nice about me. But even when Cannon did give me a good word, it would only be for himself or because I'd got him a win bonus: normally he wouldn't give me the time of day. But with Tony, it's just the highest amount of respect I can give a man: he's a natural born leader and should be the captain of England, no matter who is in the team.

And Paul Ince should be in the same team, shoulder to shoulder with Tony, because they're cut from the same cloth. Incey and I go closer than two footballers – we're more like brothers after everything that we've shared over the years, and there's so much respect between us. I didn't really know him before the FA Cup Final where Palace drew with Manchester United, but afterwards he came up and shook hands and said, 'That was blinding what you did today, coming on and scoring twice.' To hear that from the opposition and from somebody I had so much respect for was really special. We connected that day and there was something about him that I really admired. People say it's a black thing, but it's nothing to do with that. I just respect him because of his dedication and his honesty. He's a bit like Tony in that he wants everybody to play up to the standards that he sets, and if they don't he'll be right on their case.

We got to know each other on England sessions. We both had single rooms to start with but we got on so well in training and shared the same sense of humour and attitude that he moved into my room and from then on we shared. He also looks after me, and when you've got a minder like Incey, you don't need much more. He even used to have a go at Brighty when Palace played United. Brighty would be shouting at me to make a run or take up a position and Incey would say, 'Leave Wrighty alone, he's the only player that you've got,' and every other player on the pitch would look at him as if he was mad.

I think Incey's hunger comes from the fact that he nearly had to give up the game just before his transfer to Manchester United because of the problems he had with his pelvis. The realisation that everything he had worked for might have gone out of the window drives him on these days and gives him that bite. We have a lot in common, and a natural bond, and I feel as if I've known him all my life. People say you never make friends in football, only acquaintances, and 99 per cent of the time that's true. But with me and Incey, there's a special thing. The only problem with him is that he's so rough, even though I'm supposed to be a good friend, he always wants to fight. It's like tiger cubs or something like that: they can never just play – it always turns into a scrap. I picked Incey up from the airport last season to take him to an England get-together and I was just chatting in the car with another guy when Incey suddenly punched me in the mouth. There was no provocation, nothing – he just wanted a test of strength, so he and I went for it in the back seat of the car. Afterwards my lip was bleeding, his teeth were bleeding and we were just sitting there laughing like a couple of fools!

Paul will not suffer idiots at any price. If we're out and punters come up and ask us for autographs or to pose for pictures, he'll do it gladly. But if after we've done it the geezers are still hanging round hoping to be included in the conversation, he won't have any of it. He'll turn round and say, 'Listen, we've done what you wanted, now can you give us a bit of privacy because we're just trying to have a drink and relax.' He knows the guy will go back to his mates and not tell them how he's got these autographs and pictures, just how Paul Ince told him to get lost. That doesn't bother Incey, he just gets on with his life and never mind anybody else.

The thing that upsets me most of all is the way that Paul has been treated by England. It wouldn't matter whether I loved him like a brother or not, I would always admire him as a player. It doesn't matter what system England play, Incey should be in that team in whatever role necessary because he can fit into it. He can pass, he can tackle, he's got inspirational leadership qualities, so what the hell is against him?

There was a time quite early on last season when things weren't going right for him in Milan and it looked as though he might come back to join Arsenal, and that really excited me. To think that I might end my playing days with him behind me, backing me up and setting Highbury alight was something that would have given me a real buzz, it would have been so good.

The move to Italy tore Incey apart and I saw close up just what a nightmare he was going through. He had a great loyalty to United: they meant everything to him and I think he would have been quite happy to have spent the rest of his career at Old Trafford, even if it meant turning his back on the untold riches Inter Milan were offering. He wanted to emulate Bryan Robson and be captain of United and show people just how much he loved the club. Instead, Alex Ferguson devastated him when he said that he wouldn't stand in his way and then told the papers that the money United would get would pay for a new training ground. And Ferguson cut his heart out when he claimed that United wouldn't miss Paul because they had Roy Keane and Nicky Butt to just step in and fill his boots. Fill his boots? Don't make me laugh! I like Nicky and he's going to be a great player, but every single club in the Premiership would have given Incey a home, so don't tell me an inexperienced kid is a better player. All United had to do was ask Paul to stay and he would have, but it was clear that they didn't want him.

I was on holiday in Sardinia with Paul and his family when it was reported in the papers that Ferguson had said that Incey had manufactured his move from the moment they lost the FA Cup Final to Everton. I couldn't believe what I was reading and the pain it caused Paul was dreadful to witness. He didn't know which way to turn because he knew that he couldn't leave Manchester on such a low note with all the fans thinking he was like a rat leaving a sinking ship. The place where we stayed in Sardinia is one of the most beautiful places in Europe, but for two weeks we hardly noticed it because Paul was going through such emotional turmoil. He was so disappointed, let down and confused. I tried to lift him and tell him that Italy was a wonderful opportunity and a chance to see a different culture, but I knew in my heart that all he wanted was for Ferguson to pick up the phone and say, 'Come back son, everything will be all right.'

People know how close I am with Incey and Brighty, but what they don't often realise is how close I am with Tony Finnigan. We've kind of grown up together, we're both from south London and our whole families know each other and get on well. He could come to my mum's house and she would treat him like one of her own sons and exactly the same with me and his family. There's a bond between us that has been strengthened after an incident involving Tony and the police. What happened was, he was done for possessing a minute amount of heroin which was found in his car, but I know Tony and I can hand on heart say that there was no way he was using or dealing drugs of any kind, let alone heroin.

It was an awful time for Tony and I was proud to be able to help him out. I posted bail for him, despite the advice of some so-called friends who advised me to stay clear of the whole scene or else I might get tainted with the drugs thing. Stay clear? There was my best friend battling against a massive injustice, and people wanted me to just leave him there to fend for himself. They must have thought I was some kind of traitor who would leave his mate in the lurch just to keep his own nose clean.

I felt very angry and upset with Bruce Rioch over one incident which involved Finn. Tony's verdict was due on the Monday lunchtime and I wanted to be there, just to show that I was with him, but because Bruce had the hump that I'd spent a free weekend filming an advert for Nike in Tunisia, he put the block on it. I phoned Gary Lewin and asked if it was all right if I missed the morning session but trained in the after-noon. Now I have never pulled a moody to miss a training session in my life, even when I'm injured I still like to be out there because I just love training. I was more than willing to put in the hours in the afternoon but Bruce said no, it wasn't possible. That was fair enough, but as I was trying to get away quickly from the training ground, Bruce shouted out that I had to come back for an afternoon session.

I couldn't believe what I was hearing. Bruce knew how much it meant to me to be with Finn when the verdict was due and for him to turn a blind eye to that was tough to take. My 'brother' needed me there, he'd asked me to be there and I'd let him down, which made me feel terrible.

The fact that I wasn't there hasn't spoiled our relationship because Tony got the result that I knew he would, but if it had gone the other way, I'm not sure how he would have reacted to me going missing. We're deep, far deeper than just friends, but betrayal is a terrible thing and I have seen it destroy relationships. I wasn't there when Tony needed me most and I wouldn't have blamed him if he thought I'd betrayed him.

I got close to Andy Ansah who is now at Southend when we were both at Palace. My heart went out to him because of a something that proved just how tight the gap between success and failure is in our game. He was doing well in the youth team and reserves, scoring lots of goals and really setting the place alight just at the time when the club were deciding who to take on as full professionals. I knew that Steve Coppell liked and rated him and it was only a matter of time before he signed on as a professional. But for some reason Peter Prentice, one of the scouts, took Andy to one side and without even consulting Steve said, 'Sorry son, I don't think we'll be taking you on.' Andy was devastated, he was sobbing, so I grabbed Peter and said, 'No man, that's not right, you have to see Steve.' So we went to see the boss and he said, no, of course the club were keeping Andy and he was dead impressed with what Andy had done. Now he's like a little brother to me, and Deborah and I are close to him and his young family.

It's important to me that I've got great friends: people like Incey, Brighty, Finn, Andy Ansah, Andy Gray and Mitchell Thomas, people with whom I can relax and just switch off. They're all in the same line of business so they all know the pressures that we're under, but it's very rare that we'll sit and talk football. When you get that all day at work, then you just want to escape from it, kick back and enjoy life. Being a professional footballer has given me a great life, but one thing that I treasure above everything is the fact that it has helped me meet some very special people who I can count as friends for the rest of my life.

I couldn't finish talking about my mates without mentioning the ex-great Everton footballer, no, not Bob Latchford, but the one and only Jim Pearson, now a 'great' at Nike, who have been my boot sponsors for many years.

15
A Natural
Show-Off

There comes a time when every player looks at himself and wonders what he will be doing when he quits the game. I've got to be realistic and say that in four years time I will definitely be on my way out, although I still feel I've got so much to prove and achieve in those four years. I may be 32, but I still feel as if I'm in my mid-twenties. I'm not trying to kid myself or anybody else, I genuinely do feel fit and fresh. I love training every day, and the buzz that I get when I walk out on a Saturday afternoon still gets to me every time – it's like a drug that I can't live without.

I'm still trying to make up for lost time because I came into the game so late. Take Ryan Giggs, he's still only the same age as I was when I first kicked a ball for Palace, and look what he's achieved in such a short space of time. 'Giggsy' is obviously a special case, but more and more teenagers are coming into the game and being successful as well as making bundles of dough. I do regret the fact that I kind of wasted those teenage years; I know I should have knuckled down and perhaps worked harder at my game and I might have got on the professional ladder a bit earlier.

Having said that, I'm lucky because I saw what the other side of life can be like, and a career after football will come as a shock to hundreds of players who've known nothing else but kicking a ball for a living. Thankfully, decent Premiership players shouldn't have to worry about money as much as the old professionals had to. There is a massive gap between footballers and the ordinary guy in the street as far as wages are concerned, and that gives us much more scope. I'm not knocking the old guys, but I don't think too many top players will have to depend on running a pub or becoming insurance salesmen to see them through to retirement.

I'm not being big-headed, but I know that I would never actually go out and graft to make a living when I retire. My adviser, Jerome Anderson, has made sure that I've invested a hell of a lot of money in pension plans to cater for when I retire, and I owe a huge debt of gratitude to both him and Jeff Weston who have guided me through some pretty rough times during my playing career. They've also looked after me off the pitch and made sure that I won't have to worry financially about my future.

The guy in the street must reckon that professional footballers have a cushy life, and to an extent he'd be right. We do get treated well by our clubs on the whole, we do earn a good living and we do get to enjoy the nicer things in life. But if anybody reckons that playing football for a living is anything other than work, then they ought to come and train with Arsenal for a month. Admittedly we don't slave away from eight to five every day, but the physical effort we put in must be just as great, and remember I've done both so I can make a comparison. When I say to people I've just finished work, they laugh and raise their eyebrows, but I have just as many pressures as an office worker. My career is going to be over by the time I'm in my mid-thirties, just when most people are settled on a career path and aiming to go higher and higher. Also, there's a fairly good chance that my knees and ankles are going to be knackered by the time I'm in my forties. Just look around at the players who have been retired for ten or fifteen years: I bet in the winter most of them are getting grief from their joints when the cold gets into them.

Don't get me wrong, I'm not claiming to be hard done by because we get well rewarded for playing a game we love. But if I come back as a sportsman in another life, I want to be swinging a golf club or tennis racquet because those are the boys that make the dough and have the high life. My mum used to be glued to the television during Wimbledon fortnight every year and she kept telling me and my brothers that this was the sport to be in. I almost wish I'd listened to her now. I'm good friends with Greg Rusedski, Britain's number one tennis star, and I'm green with envy when he tells me he's just back from Florida or just off to Australia or the Caribbean for some tournament or another. I know he's working very hard to make a living, but, man, give me Monte Carlo over Hartlepool any day!

I tend to get on really well with other sportsmen because there's a mutual respect for other people who have got to the top of their chosen profession, and a natural bond. Basketball is my other great love, and last season I got to meet and shoot some hoops with Hakeem Olajawon who was NBA's number one, and we got on like a house on fire. I've also met André Agassi a couple of times and he is one cool guy. God has certainly blessed that boy because to have that much talent and be that hip is very rare!

Looking beyond football is very difficult for me because I'm the happiest and most satisfied I've ever been in my life. I've got a wonderful wife in Deborah, and my son Stacey is just about one of the greatest things that has ever happened to me. He's two, and already he's turned me into something that I never thought I would be, and that's the doting father. I used to come home from training and if things hadn't gone too well then I would be absolutely insufferable. Deborah would seriously stay out of my way for a couple of hours because I was hell to live with when I was in a mood.

Nobody could talk to me, I used to sulk like a baby and I just didn't want to be around people. But since Stacey has come along, all that's changed. I might come home from training in a foul mood, but a couple of minutes with him and I've snapped out of it and we just play for the rest of the day. He's great to have around because it just relaxes me to be with him, and I realise that there's nothing in life worth getting worked up about.

Having Stacey around now, I realise just how much I missed not being around when my other boys grew up, and I hate to think how it must have been for them. The past is the past, but sometimes I can't help looking back and thinking how different it might have been: not better, but different. I really was too young and immature to handle my two previous relationships and I don't think I knew how to love the girls enough in the way that I love Deborah. I still get on pretty well with Sharon who is mother to Shaun and Bradley, and perhaps she was too good for me at the time because I was a bit of a rogue. I have hardly anything to do with Beverley, Brett's mum. I do everything I can for all four of my boys and I want them to grow up being proud of their father and realise that he loves them all dearly.

They all seem to be following in their father's footsteps. Shaun signed schoolboy forms with Nottingham Forest last season just after his fourteenth birthday and everything seems to be going really well for him. I think he could have quite easily signed for a London club, but being in Nottingham will help keep him out of the spotlight a little, although I know he'll always carry the baggage of having Ian Wright as a dad. Already he's come in for some attention from the papers, and I think he found that hard to handle, but he'll realise that he'll have to overcome bigger hurdles than that if he wants to be a top professional. Bradley's also attracting a fair bit of interest and one of the Arsenal scouts reckons that he's one of the brightest prospects he's seen for quite a time. I would always encourage my boys to play football, but I'd never say 'be a footballer'. I'd say 'be a top footballer': the only place to play is at the top. I don't think I could handle knowing that I was only going to be an average player – it was always the best or nothing for me. It may sound conceited and I'm not having a dig at anybody who plays outside the Premiership, but I've always had the attitude that you have to be the best or it's not worth being anything.

There's not too much that I want from life at the moment. Last year Deborah and I moved into our dream house out in Surrey which is everything that we had always wanted. It also allowed me to fulfil an ambition and have a snooker room and a full-size table. Ever since I was a kid, I'd read about rich and famous people and they'd always have a snooker room or a swimming pool in their house, and it was something that I'd always longed for. I wasn't worried about not having a pool, but when I got my table I was like a kid all over again. Now I've become addicted to it, and anybody who comes over to the house is always challenged to a game. I'm just as bad a loser at snooker as I am at football, but it's completely relaxing and therapeutic to be able to knock a few balls around the table every night.

I've realised that I've got to relax more. Looking back I wish I'd been able to chill out a bit more often, but I always wanted to be going out and doing something. Now I think it would have been better to have had a bit more time doing nothing, just being at home. Playing the saxophone was a way of just easing off the pace a bit, but just recently that's taken a bit of a back seat. My teacher is looking for a smaller alto sax because the tenor that I had was too big for me. When I was a kid I suffered pretty badly with asthma and even now my chest gets a bit wheezy, so I can't reach the very low notes on the tenor. When I get my alto I'll get back into the swing of the sax and maybe get some piano lessons for Stacey so we can jam together.

Music and fashion have always played a major part in my life. When I was at school, the most important things were how well you could play football, what music you were into and what clothes you wore. Deep down, I've never ever lost those values. I made a record a few years back called 'Do the Right Thing' with Chris Lowe from the Pet Shop Boys, and I've got to say that satisfied a lot of ambitions. I've always wanted to be up there performing, no matter what I'm doing, because I'm a natural show-off, although not a brazen one! Football is performance, music is performance and when you go out, you're up there on a stage as well. That's why I love going out and buying clothes: it's one of my major hobbies. I've always prided myself on looking good and looking different. Why be part of the crowd when you can be an individual? There are certain things that I do just to be different, like wearing my collar tucked in on my Arsenal shirt and having a Harley Davidson tattooed on my thigh. They're only small things but I just feel compelled to do them to stand away from the crowd.

Although I feel totally settled in my football career and I'm so happy with my home life, there's still a part of me that has got itchy feet. What Deborah and I talk about a lot is that I've been in relationships all my life: I've bounced from one serious relationship to another and never spent any real time on my own. That always creeps up when Deborah and I are talking about the future. I know it's a dead selfish thing to say but sometimes I wish I'd lived that single life where you don't have quite so many responsibilities, you're not governed by anybody else and you just have time and space to settle your mind on what you want to do. I never, ever want to lose what I've got with Deborah, Stacey or my other boys, but there's still that nagging feeling at the back of mind that just wants that solitary life. God willing, it will never happen, but it would be interesting to see how I would handle it and what I would be like as a person.

That forms one of my last remaining ambitions. When I pack in football, I'd love to just take six months out of my life and drive coast to coast across America on a Harley just to be out there on my own fending for myself. At the moment, if anything crops up, I can just buy myself out of it, and I'm lucky to be in that sort of position. But I want to test myself, I want to see if I can handle life without all the benefits that I've got at the moment just to see how I would cope. It's a pipe dream because I don't think that I could ever live without Deborah or Stacey. In fact, it's a childish thing because I look at myself and say, 'How the hell can you do that? You've got a wife and four kids to look after.' But we all have to have dreams, even if we'll never fulfil them.

I'm not seeking anything, but I do want to break away from the run-of-the-mill type of things that people do. Footballers are a strange breed because we've always had things done for us, decisions made for us, and all we have to do is turn up. We're told what time to report for matches, what we'll be eating and even what we have to wear, and now I feel like rebelling against that, even if it's in a small way. I don't want to go on the usual sun and beach holiday even though I know I can afford to go to some of the greatest places in the world. I want to go somewhere away from civilisation where you have to just get in touch with the people who live there and, in a way, get in touch with yourself. The one thing that playing for England has done for me is to make me appreciate the places that we visited. I don't mean America and Spain and those sort of places: I mean Albania, Poland and Russia where the culture is so different to what we're used to in England. When I see people who have nothing and no likelihood of life getting better, it makes me appreciate how lucky I am. So the very least I can do every Saturday is try and run myself into the ground to show people how much that I appreciate being God blessed at being able to play football for a living.

Football has been brilliant to me, but I know there's no way that I will stay on in the game when I quit playing. One thing's for certain: I'm not cut out to be a manager. I don't want the hassle of dealing with players and I certainly don't have the patience to be able to take a training session. I'm not the best tactical player – tactics bore the life out of me because I have no appreciation of them. I'm an instinctive player who does things off the cuff, and those sort of players have never made great coaches or managers. Can you imagine me dealing with authority as a manager? I'd be out of the game before the end of my first season, either run out by Lancaster Gate or having jacked it in myself because I'd be banging my head up against a brick wall!

I would love to be a football pundit on the television and I'll tell you something, I wouldn't be one of those guys who get splinters up their rear ends by sitting on the fence. I would want to be somebody in the mould of Sky's Andy Gray because I respect every single word that he says. Without him, Sky would be average, but he's like a shining beacon of truth and honesty in a world where people sometimes only say things to impress others or keep them happy. I want to be like him: I want people to sit there and say, 'That Ian Wright talks a lot of sense. When he explains things I really understand it.' Andy is like that. We were sitting at home with my cousin one time and she knows nothing about football, but when Andy pointed out something she immediately cottoned on and appreciated the incident and that is a gift. I want people to value my opinion and realise that I am always talking from the heart, even if it sounds disrespectful at times.

This book has been a way of doing that, and all I want is for people to read it and realise that I try to be 100 per cent honest in everything that I've ever done, in football as well as life. I'm no saint, I'm just an ordinary guy who has been privileged to play football for a living. It's a great life and I thank God I've had this opportunity.

Career highlights

1963: Born 11 November to father Herbert and mother Nesta at the Royal Military Hospital in Woolwich, London. Older brothers Morris and Nicky and younger sister Dionne.

1973: Star striker for Turnham School, South London.

1977: Rejected after South London Schools trials, a side that also included future Palace team-mate Andy Gray.

1978: Trials with local side, Millwall, but again rejected.

1981: Signs for his first men's team, Ten Em Bee in the London and Kent Border League and is an immediate success, topping the scoring charts in the league.

1982: Trials with Brighton and Hove Albion. Rejected again, despite scoring for the reserves.

1985: After several outstanding seasons with Ten Em Bee, is invited to sign for Greenwich Borough. Also has trials with non-league Dulwich Hamlet, where is spotted by Palace scout Peter Prentice and invited for a two-week trial at Selhurst Park. After just three days, Steve Coppell offers him a three-month contract at £100 a week. Makes his debut for Palace on 31 August in the 3–2 home defeat by Huddersfield. Scores his first senior goal on 10 October as Palace beat Oldham 3–2. Ends the season with nine goals from 32 appearances.

1986: A regular in an average Palace side and still to discover the sensational scoring form that would mark him out as a future international.

1987: Scores 20 league goals for the first time in his career as a devastating partnership with Mark Bright develops.

1988: Signs a new contract with Palace despite the fact that both Liverpool and Spurs are rumoured to be interested.

1989: Palace win promotion to the (old) First Division through play-offs, beating Blackburn at Selhurst Park 3–0 with Ian scoring twice after losing the first leg at Ewood Park 3–1. A few months later, he scores his first goal in the top flight as Palace draw 1–1 with Manchester United. In December Ian makes his England B debut against Yugoslavia at the The Den.

1990: A broken leg against Liverpool but Ian is back six weeks later to help Palace beat Cambridge in the FA Cup quarter-finals. Two games later, he breaks his leg for a second time in the match against Derby and is forced out of Palace's semi-final with Liverpool at Villa Park, which the underdogs clinch 4–3 in extra time. Ian is fit for the final against Manchester United but is kept on the bench until the second half, when he comes on to score twice and put Palace ahead. Mark Hughes scores in the last minute to force a replay, where Ian again starts on the subs bench but cannot repeat his feat of four days earlier and United win 1–0.

1991: Palace are back at Wembley and Ian scores as the Eagles beat Everton 4–1 in the final of the Zenith Data Systems Trophy. Picked by Graham Taylor in February and makes his full international debut at Wembley for England's friendly with Cameroon. England win 2–0. After six outstanding seasons with Palace and over 200 goals, George Graham pays a then Arsenal record of £2.5 million to take him to Highbury and two days later, Ian repays the first chunk of that fee with a goal on his debut against Leicester in the Coca-Cola Cup. Becomes an immediate Highbury hero with a hat-trick against Southampton on his league debut for the Gunners the following Saturday. Ends the season as Arsenal's top scorer with 24 goals in just 30 league appearances. Makes three further appearances for England, coming on as a sub against the Republic of Ireland and starting the games against Russia and New Zealand.

1992: Ends the season as Britain's top goal-scorer, pipping

Lineker by just one goal, yet is overlooked by Taylor for the European Championships in Sweden, a young and untried Alan Shearer going instead. As the new season starts, Ian rubs salt into Taylor's wounds as his goals propel Arsenal to an amazing double Wembley feat 12 months later. The down side of the year is his record fine and ban after being found guilty of hitting Tottenham's David Howells.

1993: Still not the main man in the England set-up despite a phenomenal scoring record for Arsenal. Becomes the quickest player to 100 goals for the Gunners, beating Ted Drake's 40-year-old record. Arsenal make it to the final of both the Coca-Cola and FA Cup where, incredibly, they twice meet Sheffield Wednesday. Ian fails to score in the League Cup but grabs Arsenal's goal in the 1–1 drawn first FA Cup final. Scores again in the replay as Arsenal win 2–1 thanks to Andy Linighan's goal in the last minute of extra time. Ian finally breaks his duck for England, scoring the vital goal against Poland in Chorzow and giving Taylor's side an invaluable draw. Ian marries Debbie Martin in June on the Caribbean island of Necker.

1994: England fail to qualify for the World Cup in America. Taylor's sacking and the appointment of Terry Venables virtually mean the end of Ian's international career. At club level, Arsenal struggle in the league but are blazing a trail in Europe as they start their Cup Winners' Cup campaign. Disaster strikes for Ian in the semi-final second leg against Paris St Germain at Highbury, when he is booked for a second time in the competition, missing the final where Arsenal beat Parma 1–0. In June, Ian's fourth son, Stacey, is born.

1995: Scandal hits Highbury as George Graham is accused of taking 'bungs' from transfers and Paul Merson admits to being an alcoholic and to snorting cocaine. Graham is later sacked and suspended for a year while Merson is rehabilitated and returns to Arsenal. On the pitch, Arsenal are only just above the relegation zone yet Ian still scores prolifically, especially in Europe where he finds the back of the net in every one of Arsenal's ties, equalling Ferenc Puskas's 30-year record. His incredible streak comes to an end in the final in Paris where Arsenal are beaten by Real Zaragoza in the last seconds of extra time. Bruce Rioch takes over as Arsenal manager and immediately there are stories about a clash between him and Ian.

1996: Ian stuns Highbury and the football world by handing in a transfer request, claiming it is in his and the club's best interests if he quits Arsenal. The Highbury board turn down the request despite interest from Chelsea and Ian sees out the rest of the season with Arsenal.

SUMMARY
(up to the end of the 1995/96 season)

CRYSTAL PALACE
League appearances 225
League goals 90
L/Cup appearances 19
L/Cup goals 9
FA Cup appearances 11
FA Cup goals 3
Other appearances 22
Other goals 16

ARSENAL
League appearances 162
League goals 95
L/Cup appearances 25
L/Cup goals 23
FA Cup appearances 14
FA Cup goals 12
Other appearances 18
Other goals 15

TOTAL
League appearances 387
League goals 185
L/Cup appearances 44
L/Cup goals 32
FA Cup appearances 25
FA Cup goals 15
Other appearances 40
Other goals 31

ENGLAND
20 caps (including 10 as sub)
5 goals
B caps 3

HONOURS
ZDS Trophy 1990/91
FA Cup 1989/90 (runners up)
1992/93
Coca-Cola Cup 1992/93
European Cup Winners Cup 1994/95 (runners up)

Index